Leading
Product Development

Leading
Product Development

The Senior Manager's Guide to
Creating and Shaping the Enterprise

Steven C. Wheelwright
Kim B. Clark

THE FREE PRESS
New York   London   Toronto   Sydney   Tokyo   Singapore

The Free Press
A Division of Simon & Schuster Inc.
866 Third Avenue, New York, N.Y. 10022

Printed in the United States of America

printing number

1 2 3 4 5 6 7 8 9 0

Library of Congress Cataloging-in-Publication Data

Wheelwright, Steven C.
    Leading product development / Steven C. Wheelwright, Kim B. Clark.
        p. cm.

    1. Industrial project management.   2. New products—Development.
    I. Clark, Kim B.   II. Title
    T56.8. W47   1995
    658.5'75—dc20   94–41392
                                                                  CIP

Credits for figures reproduced or adapted from previous books are as follows:

Figures 1–1, 3–2, 5–2, and 5–5: *Revolutionizing Product Development* by S. C. Wheelwright and K. B. Clark. Copyright © 1992 by Steven C. Wheelwright and Kim B. Clark.

Figures 2–1 and 6–1 (identical): *Revolutionizing Product Development* by S. C. Wheelwright and K. B. Clark. Copyright © 1992 by Steven C. Wheelwright and Kim B. Clark. *Dynamic Manufacturing* by R. H. Hayes, S. C. Wheelwright, and K. B. Clark. Copyright © 1988 by The Free Press. Reprinted with permission of The Free Press, a Division of Simon & Schuster.

ISBN-10: 1-4165-7634-7
ISBN-13: 978-1-4165-7634-1

To our students,
who teach us as they tackle the challenges of leadership.

Contents

Preface   vii

Acknowledgments   xi

1. The Leadership Challenge   1

2. A New Role for Senior Management:
   From Problem to Solution   21

3. Less is More: Building an Effective Project Portfolio   47

4. Creating Consistently Effective Project Teams   75

5. Leadership in Action:
   Developing Single-Use Cameras at Kodak   103

6. Turning Promise into Reality   135

   Additional Readings   165

   Index   171

   About the Authors   177

Preface

The publication of our book *Revolutionizing Product Development* (New York: Free Press, 1992) marked the culmination of years of research and course development on product development in a number of companies, industries, and countries. In *Revolutionizing* we laid out the frameworks, concepts, tools, and methods that had proved powerful in driving superior performance in lead time, design quality, and development productivity. Since that time, we have continued to teach hundreds of senior executives, to work with many companies as they implemented these ideas and concepts, and to do research and case writing on the development of new products. Our experiences have confirmed the power of the ideas in practice. We have seen numerous companies in a variety of industries achieve dramatic improvement in speed, quality, and productivity by adapting and applying the concepts and methods presented in *Revolutionizing*. As one senior executive in a highly competitive industry noted, "If a company did everything in that book, it wouldn't have any competition."

It has been exciting for us to see the impact of these ideas, yet we have been struck by a recurring paradox. Senior management, deeply aware of the need for substantially improved product development performance and enthusiastic in its desire to launch new initiatives, takes action to implement these new concepts (such as development strategy, aggregate project plans, cross-functional integration, and heavyweight teams) and then anxiously awaits the results. After initial success with a demonstration project or two, however, the realization sets in that sustained success requires consistent excellence in *every* project, and thus pervasive change in the *entire* organization—including what senior management does. And this is where senior managers begin to feel frustrated and uncertain about their own role in the process. Time and time again we have heard them lament that the skills and actions on which they relied in the past—taking charge, pushing for more, or saving the day at the eleventh hour—no longer seem effective when the broader picture must be considered. Indeed, at times such measures appear counterproductive.

As new approaches to planning, teams, and cross-functional integration have taken hold in business, it has become apparent that senior management's role must change in fundamental ways. Understanding the concepts and introducing them to the organization is not enough. Indeed, for sustained success in improving product development, even strong, well-intentioned support of (or, moreover, deep involvement in) a new approach to product development is insufficient. Senior managers must take action in a different way; they need to play a new role.

Our research and our direct experience with hundreds of executives have convinced us that the key to consistently excellent performance in product development is senior management leadership. What is needed is a new framework for action that focuses specifically on senior managers and their role in leading product development. And so, we set out to write this book.

Leading Product Development is written for senior managers—

those people charged with running the business. Throughout the book, when we speak of senior managers or senior management, we have in mind a business led by a group of senior executives that includes the president or general manager as well as the heads of the major functions (marketing, operations, engineering, human resources, finance, customer service, and so forth). We have written *Leading* as a companion volume to *Revolutionizing; Revolutionizing* presents an in-depth analysis of the tools, concepts, and frameworks necessary for rapid, productive, high-quality development, while *Leading* focuses on the role of senior management in leading that process. Senior managers who take the framework for action to heart and grasp and apply the ideas we present here will reap the rewards. This is not a theoretical book. It is grounded in practice, and the ideas work.

Acknowledgments

Many people have helped us write this book. We are especially indebted to the hundreds of senior managers whom we taught and interviewed, and with whom we discussed and debated the challenge of leading product development. They shared their insights and experiences, provided access to their businesses, and encouraged and supported our search for a leadership framework. We have been very fortunate to work with some truly outstanding senior managers in many different industries, types of businesses, and countries.

As in all of our work, we have benefited from the encouragement and support of our colleagues at the Harvard Business School. From the very beginning, Dean John McArthur encouraged us to set our sights high and was unwavering in his support. We are grateful to Warren McFarlan and the Division of Research for the resources to do this work, and to our colleagues in the Technology and Operations Management area for their insights, colleagueship, and friendship. HBS is simply a wonderful place to work, and this book is all the better for it.

Acknowledgments

We also want to thank Natasha Omdahl, Jean Smith, and Barbara Feinberg for helping us turn ideas into reality. Natasha took on the task of keeping our academic lives on track while we immersed ourselves in writing. She also helped on the manuscript with skill and good spirits. Jean, as always (this is her fourth book with us), was instrumental. She produced the manuscript, handled the graphics, edited the text, and generally kept us on our toes throughout. Barbara was our editor, but her work went far beyond the editorial. She encouraged, pushed, and prodded us to sharpen, clarify, and *integrate* our ideas, concepts, and themes. She helped turn rough, semicoherent (and sometimes rambling) prose into crisp, clear English. Moreover, she did all this with great skill and enthusiasm. We are grateful for her commitment.

Finally, we owe a special thanks to our families for their patience and support as we worked on what we found exciting and challenging. They kept us anchored to reality and the things that matter most.

1
The Leadership Challenge

Whether it is a Pentium chip from Intel or a birdhouse with a "Spanish tile roof" from Rubbermaid, the successful new product both satisfies and delights customers. It conforms to an increasingly broad range of customer expectations about quality and design as well as delivery and service performance; at the same time, it introduces something different—a new dimension of functionality, a new feature, something unanticipated in the "package of benefits" provided. For companies such as Intel and Rubbermaid, in industries as seemingly disparate as state-of-the-art ICs and mundane plastic household goods, new product development is at the heart of their business.

But one successful new product does not build a successful, enduring enterprise. In today's savage competitive environment, enduring success requires *consistent* excellence in developing new products. The one-shot successful deal is just that—it leads nowhere and its impact on the bottom line is fleeting in a world where the demand for new products is relentless.

Much has been done in recent years to create new methods and frameworks for making product development faster, more efficient, and more effective. Outstanding firms such as Intel and Rubbermaid have adapted a host of these new tools and techniques and felt their impact. But putting new product development at the heart of the business and achieving consistent excellence in the development of new products is not just a matter of the right tools and techniques or the latest methods and frameworks, powerful as they may be. What counts here—and what is so often hidden and undervalued—is the leadership of senior management.

Senior managers have the benefit of a rare vantage point. They see the whole of the enterprise and its future, and thus they are in a unique position to understand the importance of product development to the success of the business. When senior managers lead, they recognize the power of product development and their role in it. They understand that:

- The consequences of product development have a direct impact on competitiveness. They mean the difference between falling behind a leading competitor in the marketplace and being the competitor who provides leadership, compelling others to meet similar standards.
- The bulk of a company's assets are tied up in how it delivers value to its customers. If it has old products, the wrong products, or even the right products at the wrong time, that value is severely limited. If the firm "does" product development badly, its assets—particularly its equity with its customers—will wither and erode.
- The success or failure of product development is driven by the entire range of functions and activities—every dimension—of the organization. The development of a new product is the development of every aspect of the business that the product needs to be successful. And consistently successful new products need every aspect of the business working in harmony.

- Product development is the means by which a company *builds* capabilities. Through new product development, an organization creates the "energy"—the skills, processes, knowledge, and motivation—that drives its future. Put another way, these capabilities become the resource pool it draws from to meet future customer requirements. Thus, when product development becomes central to the business, it becomes a self-renewing wellspring of capabilities.
- Effective senior managers recognize that their most important contribution is their cumulative impact, rather than their influence on any single project. They act on the development process as a whole.
- Senior management touches everything the company does; what senior managers do sets the pattern and example for everyone in the business. Senior managers have a decisive influence on functional integration and the building of capability. Whether the business achieves integrated solutions in the short run and critical capacity for action in the long run depends on senior management leadership.

The Problem

Few senior managers would argue that new product development is unimportant; fewer still would imply that it is unrelated to "mainstream" business issues. However, the actions of many suggest that new product development is neither at the heart of their business nor central to their personal agenda. The critical issue is whether senior management *leads* product development so that developing new products is a primary focus of attention and commitment throughout the organization. The following kinds of comments are typical when product development is not a critical issue for senior management:

"Product development? We have a very talented product development group; their department is on the far side of the building. We've recently increased their budget, added some bright young people, and put in some new workstations. Product development is a priority here."

"Product development? We've organized a senior management review committee that meets monthly to monitor progress on the projects under way. Our staff helps prepare the background for these meetings, and then we ask the tough questions. When the folks working on product development don't have good answers, we send them back to the drawing board."

"Product development? Well, our budget in that area is about 4% of revenues, and that's better than most in our industry. Our chief technical officer manages the area and requests help from others as needed. So far, his group has done a great job of maintaining our image as an innovator."

"Product development? We've got a lot of sophisticated, hot new products under way—they're what our customers seem to want. Because these are highly technical and aimed at leading customers, we have our best people in R&D and marketing involved. My job is to help select projects and allocate resources, and then get out of the way. I believe firmly in delegation, lending support when it is requested and occasionally intervening if things get off track."

"Product development? Well, as the chief operating officer, my principal focus is on day-to-day operations. But from time to time, a project does get my personal attention. Especially when it threatens our corporate performance. Then, I roll up my sleeves and really dig in. Decisions—hard decisions—have to be made, and only I can make them."

On the surface, the senior managers behind these quotes are doing things to help product development. They are investing in new equipment, setting up processes to provide senior management input, employing their very best people, and empowering people to act. All are well intentioned, all are doing some things well, and all are involved in product development. But below the surface, there is something missing, and—in most cases—what is missing is very significant.

These senior managers have set limits on product development and delegated significant responsibility for its success. Product development is not at the heart of their agenda, and they do not lead. They may look at projects at a handful of key decision-making points, for example, when resources are required or when major milestones (or calendar dates) are reached. Senior managers at these points may step in to be a project's patron saint, or at least a cheerleader. But this is not enough. Although many efforts in such businesses are conceived in a spirit of hopefulness and enthusiasm, all too many end up with insufficient resources, missed deadlines, inadequate performance, and burned out, disappointed project participants. Senior managers wind up fighting fires and trying to save the day at the eleventh hour. Simply put, good intentions and close involvement will not do the job.

Because product development is so difficult to do well, the plain fact is that it needs far more timely, comprehensive, coherent action by senior management. What makes development so hard is precisely what makes doing it well so rewarding:

• *Product development touches everything the business does.* By the time a new product reaches the market it will have passed through every function, to one degree or another, in the business. Put another way, as a firm develops a new project, it is basically simulating the entire business. It must think about how the product will be manufactured, what sourcing will be involved, what the supplier chain will look like, who will be involved in distribution, and how the new product will be promoted and serviced. Additionally, the firm must think about how customers and competitors will view and experience the product and, crucially, how it will fit into the product line.

• *What matters exists in an uncertain future.* Product development necessarily entails uncertainty—about competitors, about technology, about the organization's ability to execute, and, most important, about customer acceptance of something that will arrive in the future. This last is the most vexing, for so often a product's acceptance or rejection lies in the details and specifics. Say a business wants to introduce a new "anti-aging" face cream. It invests heavily in the chemical formulation it will put in the jar. But the customer's experience is also determined by all sorts of details about the product's packaging, fragrance, aesthetics, feel, and color, its consistency and quality in production, how it is sold and where, and above all, how it is advertised. All of these details must work together as a total system. And all this has to be anticipated and addressed anywhere from several months to several years in advance.

Coping with complexity and uncertainty in an individual project is hard enough. Here the challenge is to achieve excellence in product development consistently. This calls for senior managers who can see the business as a whole, clarify what needs to be done, and pull the organization together to make it happen. Unfortunately, the pressures senior managers confront and their own instincts often get in the way of effective action. Thus, not only is product development flat out hard to begin with, but natural tendencies in senior management make it even harder.

• *The pressure is on to respond to competitors— immediately.* Pressure can come from many sources within the organization. When driven by senior managers, its consequences by and large are more immediate—and pervasive. Consider, for example, a senior manager who visits a major customer. During the conversation, the customer asks, "Why don't you have a purple square one? We get our purple square ones from Company X, your competitor. If you had one, we'd buy yours." This is brand-new information to the senior manager, who returns to the office, hauls in the development folks, pounds the table, and demands: "Why don't we have a purple square one?" Sure enough, pretty soon a project to develop a purple square one is under way.

Perhaps the senior manager also visits a key supplier, who notes, "We're on this project to incorporate a new material—of course it's for one of your competitors, but boy, this stuff is terrific." Back at the office, the development folks are ordered, "We've got to make use of this new material. We've got to get that technology; it's where the competition is going." That project, too, enters the pipeline, and the result is a hodgepodge of efforts under development.

• *The illusion of activity.* This problem exacerbates all the others. Senior managers want to ensure that people are productive, that action is being taken, that things are happening. This can be summed up as "more is more." Thus, in the absence of a sufficiently comprehensive and strategic process for evaluating what should become a project and why, the bias is to keep on adding projects—both to ensure that "things happen" and to demonstrate responsiveness to customers' wishes and competitors' threats. When there is activity, the organization looks productive. The illusion of activity, however, is deadly. It leads to scattershot efforts, badly focused resource allocation, and overloading of resources. Everything in the pipeline is jeopardized. In the end, "more is less."

• *Projects are where the action is.* In companies without strong connections between business strategy and development projects, projects become places where important issues are resolved. To keep the business on the right course, senior managers feel compelled to make key decisions. But they often slow a project down or come into it late, when the project has veered off track. The result is heroic firefighting—something senior managers often enjoy and at which they excel. But although such activity does put out fires, it does not build capability or deliver distinctive value to the marketplace.

All of these problems are evident in the tale of Global Electronics, a disguised case history that reflects an all too common reality.

Global Electronics' Compact Disc Project

The marketing group of the personal stereo systems unit at Global Electronics, a large international consumer electronics company, was concerned that a key competitor was working on a new portable compact disc system and that Global would have to respond quickly to meet this challenge. The personal systems product manager presented a concept development plan to the head of marketing for a new, competitive system that would be more sophisticated and make use of better technology. The plan indicated a project development cycle time of one year, running from September to September, thereby allowing volume production to meet expected Christmas demand (see the initial row of Figure 1–1 for the original time line). With the strong support of marketing, senior management signed off on the concept development plan for the product (code-named Falcon), and prospects looked bright.

Things began to go wrong from the outset and only got worse. First, the concept development stage was completed six weeks late because of significant disagreements about what features Falcon should have and where it should fit in the product line; no change was made to the commercial introduction schedule to reflect this early delay (see Figure 1–1 for the updated time line). Furthermore, eight weeks were added to the prototype build and test

Figure 1–1
The Falcon Time Line

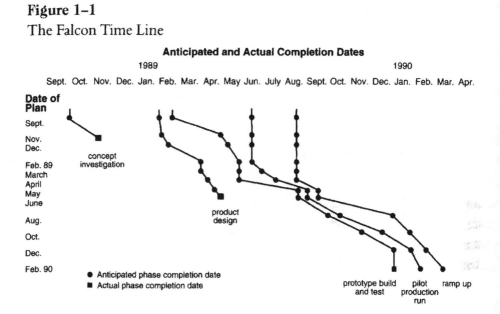

Anticipated and Actual Completion Dates

schedule because the engineering group decided to use a new signal processing chip and identified several additional technical challenges during the concept development stage.

Not long after concept development, other problems with design deadlines emerged (there was limited capacity in the drafting department), and the design completion and prototype/test schedules were revised; however, no revision was made to pilot or ramp-up schedules because everyone agreed that pre-Christmas introduction was essential. Meanwhile, even though the design was not finished, process engineering and manufacturing groups began work on the manufacturing process.

A month after the revised deadline for design completion passed, design engineers were still hard at work, wrestling with a new set of problems related to product weight and cost. Concerns about weight had surfaced in market research, and new targets had been set following the introduction of Global's XR22, a midrange product, just a few months earlier. Marketing felt that Falcon had to be priced only $50 above the XR22 to fit in the product line. At the same time, new prototype and production process difficulties emerged. Two key product engineers had been pulled off Falcon to handle a crisis during the launch of the XR22 (the disc changer mechanism was damaging the CDs), and work on the Falcon prototypes was essentially put on hold for the three weeks they were gone. For its part, process engineering was grappling with delays in tooling as it received a steady stream of engineering change orders to deal with modifications to Falcon's cost and performance. Prototype completion was rescheduled for August and pilot production and ramp up would swiftly follow: the final September date was still in effect, in part because no one working 80-hour weeks on the project wanted to be the messenger who brought such a significant date change—one that meant missing the Christmas market—to senior management.

More problems subsequently appeared, primarily because the product design and the new automated assembly equipment did not work together successfully. The equipment had been specified and installed by manufacturing to meet cost targets and reduce variable costs, but it needed extensive debugging and some of its characteristics conflicted with those of the product design. These problems only surfaced at the prototyping phase, however. As a result, the original project deadline was missed, along with the Christmas season. Prototype testing was finally completed the following February.

At this point, the product's "aesthetics" were deemed out of date (competitors had introduced new products); in response, marketing pushed through a redesign of the packaging, which meant that engineering needed a crash program entailing new tooling and testing. The redesigned product finally went into production in late summer. Meanwhile, manufacturing was debugging the redesigned assembly equipment (to deal with the packaging redesign) and testing for quality. In September, one year later than planned, volume production geared up to meet that year's Christmas season. Demand, while adequate, hardly matched original expectations; worse, design engineering and manufacturing soon faced quality problems from the field (the new manufacturing process and the design were not as complementary as planned), and these led to more engineering change orders, particularly to improve manufacturability. As a consequence, design engineering launched yet another crash program to improve quality and reliability.

Looking back, the Falcon was a challenging project, but the complexity and uncertainty it faced differed little from that of scores of projects Global had completed over the years. In fact, the Falcon experience was not atypical. Veterans at Global could recount story after story about projects that met a similar fate. Behind much of the history of poor performance (and behind the poor performance of Falcon) lay the attitudes and behavior of senior management. Believing that more is more, they had loaded a project into an overstressed organization, failed at the outset to connect it fully to the business strategy or even to other products in the line, did not give it the resources it needed, failed to recognize the need for new skills, added even shorter time requirements, and changed direction midstream in response to competitors' moves. While each of these factors could have been handled individually, collectively they spelled pain and disappointment.

Of course, there were many other problems behind the design changes, tooling delays, prototyping errors, and mismatch between the design and the manufacturing process. But of all the problems Falcon confronted, its basic difficulty was that the various pieces of the project puzzle—from the project's intent to its execution— were never considered as a whole and effectively integrated. When considered in isolation, the idea behind the Falcon—to confront the competitor's threat with a more technologically sophisticated product—seemed reasonable. But Falcon could not be developed in isolation. From the standpoint of the business, Falcon had to fit into Global's product line and technology strategy and rely on the same resources demanded by other projects. Failure to address those critical connections and interactions early in the project led to delays and costly redesigns much later.

The project also suffered from a lack of integration in execution. Because actions and decisions by the functional groups were not integrated, almost everything that could go wrong did. And once things started going wrong, difficulties compounded themselves. Marketing problems beget engineering problems, design problems beget manufacturing process problems, manufacturing problems beget scheduling delays, which beget other problems and delays, and so on.

The failure of Falcon and so many projects like it was all the more frustrating because Global had such outstanding talent and so many committed people throughout the organization. One could go into any function and find examples of excellence: creative marketing, state-of-the-art technology, highly efficient process design, responsive customer service. But excellence in the parts does not automatically lead to excellence in the whole. Without significant change in the way it managed product development, and especially without new leadership from its senior management, Global was destined to repeat its Falcon experience again and again. With the right kind of leadership, however, Global could build consistent excellence into its product development, thereby creating a source of significant advantage.

"The New Product Machine"

In its February 7, 1994, issue, *Fortune* magazine named Rubbermaid "America's Most Admired Company" (it had been one of the most admired for nine years running). In its June 6, 1994, issue, *Business Week* named two Rubbermaid products, a storage shed and a tool box, bronze winners in its annual "Best Product Designs of the Year" competition. As these and other plaudits roll in, Rubbermaid continues to roll out **one new product a day**. (Interestingly, the company considers the storage shed winner in *Business Week*'s design contest a line extension, not a new product.) Rubbermaid's business goals go beyond the "one- a-day" formulation, however; they include entering a new product category every 12 to 18 months, deriving one-third of annual sales from products introduced in the previous five years, and ensuring that one-quarter of total revenues come from non-U.S. markets by the year 2000.

Rubbermaid can commit itself to such ambitious goals because it has a robust, consistently reliable product development system in place. The goals themselves provide a sense of direction to a broad development/business strategy, which is embraced at the highest level. In 1993, Rubbermaid invested nearly $142 million (funded from operations) in property, plant, and equipment to "expand capacity, improve productivity, and tool the new products needed to support future growth," according to its 1993 Annual Report. Fourteen percent of profits went toward R&D. A crucial part of this investment was devoted to developing everything from new product designs and manufacturing technologies (including computer-aided design, computer-aided engineering, and computer-aided manufacturing tools) to a Space Management System technology that helps retailers learn how best to display Rubbermaid products. These are the support systems that aid almost every new product development effort throughout the organization.

The company, from top to bottom, is *focused* on product development. As *Fortune* noted, "Even Rubbermaid top management has acquired the habit of seeing new product ideas everywhere." (Examples include senior managers' viewing an exhibit of ancient Egyptian artifacts that suggested some "new" design approaches to kitchen utensils!) At the same time, the company's team structure ensures that product line organizations are entirely absorbed by their offerings. Without such a focus, who would be dedicated to improving ice cube trays? Ice cube trays, humble as they are, can be highly profitable if you are the market leader and insist on creating projects that will enable you to remain in that position.

It is this powerful combination of senior management dedication, wise and significant resource allocation, and concentrated team effort that make Rubbermaid a "new product machine." Record earnings in 1993 not only represented the 56th consecutive year of profitability for the company, but also marked the 39th consecutive year in which its dividend per share increased.

Being Good at Product Development Makes a Difference

Companies that are good at product development have senior managers who explicitly connect development to the business strategy. They see the connections between the parts and the whole, and take action to make those connections a reality. They work together as a team, and by example foster teamwork and integration. They recognize the power of consistency in product development because they have seen its impact on growth and profitability, market position, and morale and energy in the organization. They have placed product development at the center of the business.

But senior managers who lead product development also know that consistent excellence in new products is a journey. They are acutely aware of where they have come from, how they got where they are, and where they are going. Moreover, they know they have only begun to tap the potential for success in their organization. Although it may look like they have everything figured out, they still see great room for improvement. In fact, it seems that the better they get, the more they learn about how to make things work even better.

Something like this journey is behind one of the great success stories in the annals of product development and business performance: the creation of Hewlett-Packard's DeskJet printer for personal computers. The DeskJet printer project—the starting point for HP's dominance in the market for personal computer printers—was born of a crisis: the division faced extinction if it could not come up with a successful next-generation product. As the DeskJet story below reveals, the division became adept at executing a stream of projects that built a new business. The DeskJet and its many generations of "offspring" became not only a major source of revenue and profits (as well as a significant business) for HP, but also an example of what the rest of HP's organization needed to tackle: consistent, broad-based excellence in product development that could consistently deliver a stream of outstanding products to the marketplace.

Hewlett-Packard's DeskJet Project

In 1985, HP's Vancouver division, responsible for developing and marketing "impact" printers, was in trouble. Its products were being squeezed: on the high end, expensive laser printers provided much better quality, while on the low end, dot matrix printers offered acceptable quality at a very low price—and Epson had an 80% share of the low-end market. After reviewing its entire printer line, HP's printer group senior management gave the Vancouver division a mission: concentrate on developing a low-end printer for personal and office use. Vancouver's senior management endorsed this recommendation, and began to shape a new business strategy and to define the project. This situation and subsequent events provide an opportunity to see senior management leadership in action. This was a business in need of a new strategy, new capabilities, and a new series of products. There was no hesitancy or wavering: senior management put product development at the center of the business. It was this leadership that provided focus and brought new energy and resolve to the people who had to make the future happen.

The vision that emerged at Vancouver was to create a new segment of the market—a family of products with print quality close to that of laser printers but at a price so much lower that it would virtually eliminate sales of impact and dot matrix printers for general computer use. Thus, Vancouver's leaders envisioned a future where HP (with its proprietary technology) would emerge as a formidable player in the retail end of the computer printer market. This would not be a one- or two-year effort. If successful, it would require sustained activity and achieve superior profitability over the course of a decade.

The project to realize that strategy was designed to take HP's ink jet technology and develop it into a platform that could be the basis for a whole family of products. The product targeted as the initial offering, and thus the focus of substantial effort in Vancouver, was the DeskJet printer. The concept behind the DeskJet was simple, yet powerful: a laser-quality printer for less than $1000.

The project, however, had to do more than create the DeskJet. It had to develop a line of products, and ultimately a business, that would match the dynamics of the computer industry. It therefore had to build a range of capabilities—the energy and the skills—that would lay the foundation for these products over time. And these capabilities were formidable. Vancouver needed to learn how to produce a sophisticated product in high volumes and at low cost. It had to bring its ink jet technology, previously targeted only at professional customers but used in the DeskJet product, to the retail market. And related to these challenges, it had to learn how to operate in the retail market and understand the consumer in that market.

The DeskJet, introduced in September 1987, was a significant success. The initial product came to market within the 22-month planned development schedule (much faster than the norm) and exceeded shipping rate expectations by a factor of three. HP's market share rose dramatically. Subsequent products over the years—improved variants of the basic DeskJet, including high-end color and portable versions—have been equally successful. HP has leveraged its investment in the initial DeskJet project many times over.

At every turn, senior management leadership was crucial to that success. They made the business strategy clear, linked it to the project's charter, and defined a compelling, easily understood mission for the project team. Thus, the team that executed the DeskJet project began with a common purpose that guided its efforts as the nitty-gritty work of development proceeded. Senior management set the direction and launched the team on a successful path.

But senior management leadership went beyond strategy and direction. It took specific actions to build capability for the longer term and at the same time to provide the team with what it needed for success. Its objectives were a much tighter focus on cost, deeper integration across functions, and closer links with the customer. Rather than run the project in R&D, for example, senior management elevated marketing and manufacturing to equal status on the team and co-located the core team members. It created a new manufacturing engineering group dedicated to the DeskJet, and focused it on achieving low-cost, high-volume production. Under senior management direction, the team also implemented a new approach to prototyping (earlier, more systematic, more cross-functional) and showed prototypes to retail customers—and used their reactions—very early in the project.

We do not want to leave the impression that because senior management set the direction and shaped the project, everything subsequently flowed smoothly. Like any project, this one faced myriad problems, complications, and unforeseen difficulties. But this effort, unlike its counterpart at Global Electronics, had the crucial ingredients of success: senior management leadership in articulating the business strategy and translating that strategy into a specific charter that the team could grasp and own, as well as in committing resources, managerial attention, and effort to ensure that the project fulfilled not only its immediate objective (the product) but also the longer-term aim of building capability to drive subsequent projects and build the business. These actions had a decisive impact; they set the stage for DeskJet and paved the way for other projects to follow.

As many have learned since HP's successful DeskJet project, senior management leadership is crucial to consistent excellence in product development. The most successful senior managers have radically rethought what product development signifies in their organization and recast their involvement in the process. They recognize the power of new products in competition and the central role they must play in making them happen. They understand that the success of a project is directly proportional to its relevance to business goals, how it fits with other projects under way, how carefully it has been planned at the outset, and how well it has been executed. But they also understand that to achieve such connections and performance time after time requires consistent action on their part. They recognize that if they do not lead the effort, important things simply will not get done. In short, they have put product development at the heart of the business and shouldered the responsibility of leadership.

2

A New Role for Senior Management: From Problem to Solution

In most businesses, senior managers are active in product development. At various times, in various ways, they approve projects, allocate resources, review progress, solve problems, and fight fires. But the issue in creating high-performance development is not senior management involvement, but senior management leadership. It is not activity, but effective action, that makes the difference.

Senior managers must be capable of taking effective action to create the right set of projects and to secure consistently excellent performance across projects over time. From that perspective, they have a unique vantage point: they see the business (and product development's role in it) as a whole. The challenge is to act from that vantage point—to connect product development as a whole to the strategy of the business, and to do so time after time.

Operating consistently means that senior management must play a role (or, more accurately, several roles) in a total system of development that supports, makes use of, and reinforces its lead-

Leading Product Development

ership effort. Instead, too many senior managers' role in product development is ad hoc, reactive, and poorly timed. Much of this stems from the fundamental mismatch between attention and influence depicted in Figure 2–1.

It is our experience that senior managers' *ability to influence* the outcome of development activities rarely coincides with where and when they actually *focus their attention*. Figure 2–1 shows how this works. If you divide the diagram roughly in half, the left-hand side consists of those activities that lay the foundation for projects: setting out strategy, building capability, acquiring development resources, defining objectives, and selecting projects. The right-

Figure 2–1

Timing of Management Attention and Influence in Product Development

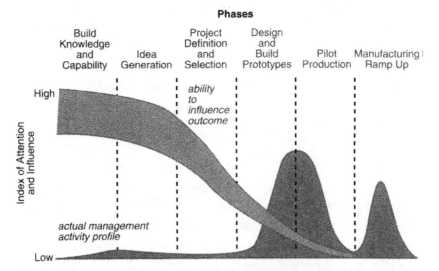

Source: S. C. Wheelwright and K. B. Clark, *Revolutionizing Product Development* (New York: The Free Press, 1992) p. 33. See also F. Gluck and R. Foster, "Managing Technological Change: A Box of Cigars for Brad." *Harvard Business Review* (1975, September–October) p. 141.

hand side covers execution of the project: setting up the teams, tracking and reviewing project status, building and testing proto-types, creating marketing plans, proving out production processes, and launching the product.

From the perspective of leading product development and achieving consistently excellent performance, the vast majority of senior management's opportunities for influence are on the left-hand side. Yet senior managers focus their attention precisely where their influence is felt least—in the execution of projects. What we have here is significant involvement, but little leadership.

The attention-influence mismatch is all too common. Powerful forces draw senior managers to the right-hand side. Often that focus is attractive, even compelling. Below is one such case drawn from a real situation, with only the names of the company and the people involved changed.

Amalgamated Inc.: The Spectrometer Division

Although the Spectrometer Division (SD) of Amalgamated Inc. had long been a leader in mass spectrometers, in early autumn 1993 it faced a changing market as critical technology matured, competition intensified, and cost and reliability grew increasingly important to customers. (In the past, SD had sold its instruments based primarily on features and performance excellence—the company prided itself on "high-end" product leadership.) To deal with the challenges of a changing environment, Joe Perina, presi-dent of SD, had embarked on a significant effort to boost growth and profitability during the prior 18 months. Division staff had been reduced, a total quality program had been launched, and manufacturing had been streamlined. Perina now felt that SD had turned the corner.

Perina's growth and profitability targets for the coming year (1994) were aggressive; at the same time, meeting them hinged on

Leading Product Development

SD's successful introduction of a new mass spectrometer, the 5000, currently under development and scheduled for introduction in June 1994. This instrument was crucial to meeting SD's projected results on sales and profitability for the third and fourth quarters of the 1994 fiscal year; it was also crucial to the division's annual growth objectives, themselves a significant part of the division's annual bonus formula. The 5000 was designed to deliver improvements in performance, along with much greater reliability and much lower cost.

In September 1993, just after he returned from vacation, Perina learned that Jim Snow, project manager for the 5000, had postponed a key design review meeting set for the following week. The meeting was to have focused on prototype test results, a critical stage in the development process. That information alarmed Perina: the previous review, in May 1993, had indicated that things were on track. Was something wrong? He called Snow, and the conversation went like this:

PERINA: Jim, what's going on with the review meeting? Why is it canceled?

SNOW: Oh, some prototype parts are late, won't be ready for a couple of weeks, and test results won't be in until late October.

PERINA: How did that happen? We're in phase 4 here—we can't be in phase 4 unless part numbers have been assigned and we're ready to build prototypes.

SNOW: Well, actually, all part numbers have been assigned, but in some cases we don't have the parts yet.

PERINA: Are you telling me that we've assigned numbers to parts that don't exist?!

SNOW: Well, yeah . . . I guess the guys figured that was the only way to keep everything on track. (Pause) We have other problems, too.

A New Role for Senior Management: From Problem to Solution

PERINA: Let me take a wild guess: marketing and R&D are arguing about the specs. Right?

SNOW: Close. Actually, they don't agree on the display subsystem. The engineers want a backlit LCD screen, but that adds about $150 to the cost, which means a $500 to $600 increase in our price once all the overhead, additional processing costs, and desired margins are factored in.

PERINA: Jim, you *know* that will kill the product. The 5000 is to be our *low-cost* instrument. That kind of a price increase will take us out of the segment—and we won't sell enough to make our budgeted share and growth projections. *What is going on?*

To find out what was going on, Perina told Snow to get his key people assembled that afternoon. He also told his assistant to "clear the decks"—cancel all but the most critical appointments and meetings, and put people on notice that he was gearing up for a major effort. Perina's instincts told him that, once again, a project was in trouble and he would have to get directly involved.

The afternoon meeting confirmed his worst fears: many parts were late, the display brouhaha was just one of many functional conflicts, and estimated costs were way out of whack. In short, not only was the project off track on timing, it seemed to be floundering. What had been, in Perina's mind, a clear direction, now seemed confused and tentative. He knew he'd have to step in and take over; the project was just too important. It needed focus—and shaking up.

Perina's initial action was to schedule a 7 a.m. meeting for Tuesday morning, and every Tuesday morning thereafter, with the key people on the project team. The first session lasted 14 hours as he and the team reviewed everything and made several major decisions. For his part, Perina made it absolutely clear that the 5000 would come out on time and that it would be the reliable, lower-cost instrument they had originally intended. It would also deliver SD's usual excellence in quality performance.

The next week's meeting lasted nine hours; within two months, the time was down to two and one-half hours. As the meeting times shortened, morale rose. The team felt it now had a "real leader." Confidence, however, was by itself not enough to solve the tough problems the project faced. So Perina took other actions.

He transferred people and authorized unlimited overtime. For example, he discovered that one bottleneck for parts was in drafting: the department was overloaded. So he met with the head of drafting, revised priorities, and put a hold on five other projects so the department could concentrate exclusively on the 5000. He also learned that Snow had been trying unsuccessfully for two months to get some people in software testing to work on 5000 protocols. So Perina stepped in and got the people assigned—he OKed subcontracting of other work and hired temporaries. What Snow had tried to do for two months, Perina accomplished in 30 minutes.

He then tackled marketing and engineering, getting them to work together on defining precisely what customers wanted from the 5000 and what the design could really deliver. He accomplished this by putting everyone in a hotel for three days of round-the-clock sessions. And it worked: they came up with a brilliant concept. The idea was to push system reliability—something Snow had been emphasizing from the outset—and cost advantage by selling the 5000 with a five-year warranty (the industry standard was 90 days). That meant additional work on software reliability, but Perina approved hiring a consulting firm to do this.

As he immersed himself in these problems, Perina thrived despite the grueling pace. He was everywhere, encouraging, probing, cheerleading, keeping everyone focused. And it paid off. The prototypes arrived in record time; within a few short months, system reliability was three to four times better than anticipated; the project got back on schedule—and then was ahead of schedule. In fact, the 5000 was introduced to lead customers for beta tests one month early. The reviews were outstanding and lead customers placed immediate orders. Subsequently, the product was introduced to the general market six weeks ahead of schedule. It was a smash hit: within six months, market share was over 15%. The division more than met its objectives and bonuses were substantial.

Perina, of course, was hailed as a hero, but he shared the glory fairly and division morale skyrocketed. In September 1994, he was promoted to COO of the entire company, considered heir apparent to the CEO.

Perina's replacement at SD, Bill Basset, a former vice president of marketing in another Amalgamated division, took over in late summer 1994 when things were on a roll. On his first day, he found a message from Joanne McNulty, vice president of marketing. He called her and introduced himself. The following conversation ensued:

BASSET: So, what I can I do for you, Joanne?

McNULTY: Bill, I'm so sorry to hit you with this on your first day, but we have to deal with this immediately.

BASSET: Deal with what?

McNULTY: Didn't you get my memo?

BASSET: All I got was a message to call you.

McNULTY: Well. . . . We've got big problems with the 5200 and the 5350. They were supposed to be ready for introduction in the fourth quarter of 1994, but there is no way we can make that date. Everyone has been working on the 5000, and we just haven't been able to stay on track with these other projects. To be frank, I don't even know where things stand with them. We haven't had a review on either for several months, and now, with the 5000 doing so well, I'm not even sure that the original plans for the 5200 and the 5350 make sense. I've tried hard to get people focused on this, but the 5000 has been like a huge gorilla. I think you're going to have to get involved—and fast.

Leading Product Development

BASSET: (Long pause) This is unbelievable! From what I understand, SD's growth plan for next year depends *critically* on these new products . . . . OK, I'll see if I can get everyone assembled tomorrow and see what's going on. Hey—thanks for the warning.

What's going on here? From one perspective, Joe Perina's efforts to save the 5000 project were admirable. He turned a seeming disaster into a triumph. He exercised leadership, and was rewarded for doing so with a promotion. From another perspective, however, the 5000 project itself reflected deep problems in the division that are just about to detonate anew, with Bill Basset now at the helm. Perina was able to get results, but only by preempting work on many other things, in many different departments, and this is now coming back to haunt the 5200 and 5350 projects. Further, although Perina got people together to push for integrated solutions that would ensure coherence within the 5000 team, these actions are what excellent *project managers* should take. Joe Perina, the division president, was an excellent project manager. But how should he be judged as a senior manager?

Senior Manager Excellence

What accounts for excellence in senior management? By and large, "excellent" senior managers are people capable not only of effective project leadership, important as that is, but of building an enterprise. That is, they are not just caretakers but architects. From our discussions with many senior leaders, and through our research, we have identified three principal ways in which senior managers specifically demonstrate excellence:

1. *They set direction and get people in the organization aligned.* Drawing on their own insights and the ideas of others in the business, they develop a sense of what is possible, articulate that vision, and work with people to align them with it. So, like an architect, they

look at the landscape and envision what could occupy it and how that could be realized. Then they work to ensure that everyone understands that vision and works for its execution.

2. *They select, train, and develop people capable of realizing that vision.* The work itself is done in projects, but it is done well only if those projects have the right people with the right skills and experience. Great senior managers attract great people to work with and for them, and they get those people through selection, training, and development.

3. Through those people, *they create, shape, and influence how work gets done in order to ensure that it gets done in the best way possible.* All senior managers own the processes by which their businesses get work done. Excellent senior managers take this ownership seriously and strive to ensure that the critical processes in their business deliver and apply the capabilities the business requires. Great senior managers fully appreciate and deeply understand the *connections* between process capability and business performance, for example, through such processes as capital budgeting, order fulfillment, personnel development, resource allocation, and product development.

If we apply the above standards to Joe Perina's approach, he comes up short. While he was an effective project leader, in his role as senior manager he not only failed to deal with the *real* project problem, he prolonged a vicious development pattern within the division. That is, the project got into a hole, so he insisted on preempting work elsewhere, including other projects; he redirected everyone's efforts to get this project out of the hole, but at the same time, ensured that more holes would appear to trap subsequent projects; and he "taught" the organization and its people that getting projects out of the hole was senior management's job.

If we return to the three "standards" above, we see:

Leading Product Development

1. *Setting direction.* Perina's first action of assembling the project team to make sure that everyone understood the product concept and what was needed to realize it was important. But doing this at the prototyping phase is very late in the day. Apparently, this crucial work had not been done successfully at the outset of the effort, insufficient attention had been paid along the way, or perhaps senior management itself had been insufficiently knowledgeable about and inconsistently committed to the project concept. The previous project review had been in May, and Perina believed that everything was fine. That things could go so wrong between then and September suggests that the senior management task of setting direction had not been accomplished.

The lack of alignment was not simply at the 5000 project level, however. Perina, for example, in his initial conversation with Snow was able to guess right away that a problem in the project was between marketing and R&D. The implication was that these *departments* were prone to feuding, and it was predictable that battles between them would be fought in the 5000 project—and, by extension, in any other development effort as well.

Perina's failure to set direction and align the troops is also implied by what happened after the initial meetings with the project team. In essence, throughout all his activities aimed at saving the 5000 project, he robbed Peter to pay Paul. This creates terrible uncertainty within an organization. No work anywhere can be performed with any assurance, for at any point everything can be put on hold, revised, and moved around. In effect, "business as usual" for SD roughly translated to "whatever the boss wants." This does not bespeak an organization whose direction is clear and whose activities and commitment are aligned to "make the future happen" through a host of concurrent development projects.

2. *Selecting and developing people.* The SD story makes clear that the 5000 project suffered from a lack of leadership. True, Perina

came in to straighten things out, and he was rewarded, quite rightly, for providing that leadership. But as noted, he was acting as a project leader. This means the designated project leader was not doing what he was supposed to do. It also means senior management was not providing leadership to ensure that project leaders were capable, qualified, and accepted by the organization to do what they were supposed to do.

Before Perina intervened, Snow may have coordinated, but he did not lead. Perina and those before him had not developed a capacity for leadership in their project managers. Furthermore, once Perina recognized the problem, he took over. He did not work through Snow, help him learn new skills, or develop new capabilities. In fact, Perina's aggressive approach made Snow look weak and ineffective. Perina may have saved the project, but he sacrificed his project leader and, by implication, future project leaders. And the way he saved the project—by preempting other projects, moving people around, changing the rules by decree—was not a model that project leaders could or should follow.

Apart from being deficient in leading projects, there is ample evidence that senior management had not taken steps to get the right kinds of people for the project. The 5000 needed to be much more reliable not just in its components, but in its software. Moreover, there needed to be a much more rigorous testing program than ever before, and issues of cost and manufacturability needed much more attention. The project needed people with skills other than the traditional approach to instrument development, but it was only after Perina's immersion in the project that those needs were fully recognized. Given the pressures of the moment, the only way to get the work done was to go outside the normal processes and "typical" people.

There were, of course, good reasons for Perina's actions. The 5000 was crucial and in trouble. By the time he got involved, there was no time to build capability in reliability engineering or cost ef-

Leading Product Development

fectiveness, to develop Snow as a leader, or to fill any of the other significant gaps in skill and ability.

3. *Shaping how work gets done, owning the processes, and connecting process capability to business needs.* When Joe Perina discovered that the 5000 project was floundering, he also revealed that he was out of touch with the project and the way work was done in his business. His was a superficial (and some would say naive) understanding of the development phases and the actual practices of the troops. He thought that by requiring engineers to assign part numbers, the system had ensured readiness to build prototypes. But under pressure to "keep everything on track" (or better said, to maintain the appearance of being on track), the engineers had simply assigned numbers to nonexistent parts.

Moreover, up to the time of the crisis, Perina had done little to even examine (let alone change) the standard development process. What had been effective when SD competed on pure technical performance was unlikely to work when time was of the essence and superior results in cost and reliability (which require much tighter integration across functions) were the name of the game. SD needed a different, more integrated process. What it got was drastic measures to "manage by exception" the inevitable crisis. As with the development of people, building a new process that the organization could apply consistently took a back seat to solving problems through brute force. Perina failed to deal with the root causes of SD's problems: why projects routinely went off track and why senior managers routinely had to come in and save the day.

The Self-Reinforcing Behavior of Traditional Product Development Approaches

The above discussion raises a two-pronged issue. Why is new product development not treated as a compelling business concern that merits the full focus of senior management attention and talent so that it can be connected—integrated—throughout the organization? In other words, if we return to Figure 2–1, why aren't senior managers devoting their attention to the issues on the left-hand side? And why are senior managers involved in product development at the "wrong" time, racing in at the end of the day to fix a situation that could have been avoided in the first place? That is, why do senior managers spend so much time on the right-hand side of the diagram? There are several self-reinforcing reasons that come into play. Consider first the lure of the right-hand side:

• *Low risk/high return.* When senior managers enter a project late in the day, the problem they have to handle has been identified: two functions cannot agree on a final specification, for example, or the prototype does not work, or a customer looking at it says, "No, that's not what I want." Whatever the issue, it is well defined and there is little risk of addressing the wrong problem.

At the same time, since the project is in a mess to begin with, if they don't succeed, there will be no real blame (people will say that "they gave it their best shot"). If they do succeed, however, the rewards will be immediate and substantial. People mired in a swamp naturally regard their rescuers as heroes, as do other senior executives. Career rewards inevitably follow organizational success.

• *It's urgent and it's visible.* Not only are the problems clear at this stage, they are in need of immediate solution. They are "real"; moreover, failure to solve them often means lost revenue soon. Operating at the right-hand side of the drawing, then, can be the only game in town.

• *Firefighting skills.* Fixing problems is what traditional senior managers are good at—what they are paid to do and are rewarded for. They have been trained for it, are comfortable doing it, and it is a compelling challenge. Further, when problems arise at this stage of the game, they cry out for solutions; they are the squeaky wheels no one can ignore. They desperately need oil and senior management is the provider.

• *It's exciting.* Working on urgent, visible, low-risk/high-reward project-related problems engenders a spirit of camaraderie, a "heat of the battle" enthusiasm. It gets the adrenaline flowing. The results are immediate, as well, and if senior managers do save the day, there is enormous satisfaction—all around.

Just as there are many good reasons for being involved in right-side issues, there are equally good and self-reinforcing reasons for *not* being involved in those on the left.

• *It's easy to be wrong.* Instead of fixing a problem that someone else has caused, senior managers are choosing among options, and these can be high-risk choices—a new material or technology, say. They can also be open-ended, and senior managers can be second-guessed every step of the way.

• *A lot of knowledge is involved.* If choices about which ideas to turn into development projects involve sophisticated options—new technologies or materials, for example, or brand-new trends in the market—senior managers may not be comfortable with their knowledge of them. Even if they were current a few years ago, they have been working on other things and may not feel up-to-date. At the same time, they may believe that deferring to people who do know—delegating—is a sign of good management.

• *Problems are less defined, and tools/roles are not clear.* In the absence of a well-defined process for front-end planning and definitive roles for senior managers in the process, it is hard to know where to begin. Both the problem and the process are ambiguous. Should senior managers sit down with "the team" for an hour every day? What are they supposed to do? Such questions rarely arise in the more concrete operating world where many senior managers are more comfortable.

• *Lack of metrics/long feedback loops.* It is hard to measure success (or failure) at the front end—in development planning—at least not for a long time afterwards. As a result, senior managers need a lot of confidence, perspective, and capability to risk making front-end decisions.

• *Absence of urgency.* A final point is that the business has multiple projects under way. As long as senior managers spend their time firefighting toward the end of another project or speeding up projects close to completion, they will, in fact, never have the time to devote to the front end of yet to be defined projects. It becomes a Catch-22. Firefighting consumes their time, which means they are not only unavailable for planning, but also not free for changing the situation.

The situation, in fact, resembles the old view of quality control. That is, when the defect became visible, quality inspectors flagged it and the rework department fixed it. They were *taking corrective action after the problem surfaced.* In the new view of quality control, of course, the problem is prevented from happening. Quality inspection has given way to quality *through process control*—and it has done so because it became a focal point of senior management attention. When quality is built into the process, not inspected in after the fact, the process is made in control and capable. The role of senior management is to create the process, the people, the strategy—the direction that ensures that quality is right the first time around. That is precisely what needs to happen in product development.

When senior managers devote their attention to the right-hand side of Figure 2–1, in effect, they are assuming the role of the rework department. Not only does this fail to solve and eliminate the reasons for the problems that need fixing (and thereby ensure that they will eventually recur), it fails to make the best use of what senior managers can actually bring to the table: a view of the whole. It is senior management that can look at how an individual project fits with business strategy, brand image, future trends, long-range goals, and so forth. And it is only senior managers who can manage the whole: the people to be assigned, the resources to be allocated, the skills, processes, and other support mechanisms to be used. In short, it is senior management that can *influence* product development by getting in at the beginning: building the development process right so all subsequent projects go right.

Senior management will never reach this point of influence if product development is delegated, is someone else's responsibility, or is deemed only a small aspect of the business. Senior managers will continually face complexities and uncertainties, last-minute heroics, and recurring failures, all of which will be, ultimately, of their own making. They will never have consistently excellent product development unless they make it their own responsibility and lead it.

Leading Product Development

To break out of the vicious cycle that pulls senior managers into the right side of the figure and away from the left, senior managers—the president of a division or head of the business, along with other members of the senior executive team working within the business—need to create a new product development role for themselves, just as they have created a new "quality" role for themselves. Senior managers must then exercise discipline to play the new role and, in a kind of bootstrapping, pull themselves away from "project management" on the right side and get themselves operating on the foundation activities at the left (see Table 2–1 for a summary of senior management's leadership roles).

The new senior management role actually consists of several roles; we have organized these around the flow of development

Table 2–1

The Leadership Roles of Senior Management

Front-End Roles	Back-End Roles
• Direction setter	• Team launcher
• Product line architect	• Energy source
• Portfolio manager	• Commitment manager
• Process owner/Creator	• Sponsor/Coach
	• Process improver

activities that begin with a gleam in someone's eye—the "great idea"—and extend through product launch and even beyond, to improving the development process based on what has been learned. These roles are not designed simply for the single project, however, but represent the fundamental aspects of leading product development overall, to ensure a stream of consistently successful projects.

Front-End Roles

• *Direction Setter.* In leading product development, just as in leading business strategy formulation, senior managers must set direction. This involves imagination, judgment, and knowledge so that the future of the business can be envisioned. This future, in turn, needs to be framed and articulated clearly, so that everyone in the organization understands where the business is headed.

• *Product Line Architect.* A critical responsibility of senior managers is ensuring that the organization develops the *right set of products* (and the associated production processes) and that these products come to market in a competitively effective sequence that is compelling to the marketplace. This is what we mean by product line architecture—and it is senior managers who collectively are the architect. It is their responsibility to determine what should be developed and in what sequence, what the connections should be between various products that effectively build brands and business identity, how products should be positioned in the market, and what pattern of customer benefits should prevail over time. Furthermore, as architects, they must also structure the production processes and their link to generations of product offerings.

Being able to make these architectural/strategic determinations requires a rich understanding of the current and future competitive environment, of the opportunities presented by evolving customer needs, and of the opportunities implied by the technology and engineering of potential (and existing) products themselves. We are not, of course, suggesting that senior managers replicate the work itself—do the detailed product design engineering, for example—but that senior management set the overall context in which the detailed work is done so as to benefit the overall business.

• *Portfolio Manager.* Behind all the front-end activities in which senior managers engage is the ability to understand the relationship between the business as an enterprise and the total set of projects undertaken. Thus, a key role for senior management is that of portfolio manager. Two portfolios are involved. The first is the range of projects actually under way or being considered for development. This set of efforts must be seen as a whole and *managed in aggregate.* To do this effectively, however, senior executives must also develop and manage a second portfolio: the collection of resources, people, skills, and capabilities—the organizational "energy"—needed to effectively execute development projects. Managing the organizational energy portfolio means that senior managers must identify, train, and develop people and build the capabilities the business needs.

• *Process Owner/Creator.* Senior management *owns* the development process; that is, it is responsible for its content and performance. As such, it needs to understand the work that must be done to conceive of, design, develop, and introduce new products. In particular, senior managers are responsible for and involved in the sequencing and execution of all the activities that go into the development of new products. This entails setting the critical milestones for evaluation, determining the flow of activities, and identifying the timing of events. In this sense, senior managers are more like an owner/operator than an absentee landlord.

Back-End Roles

Senior management's roles in the front end are dedicated to laying the foundation for effective projects. Senior managers also become involved in the right-hand side of the influence/attention drawing (Figure 2–1) but in a very different way than illustrated by Perina at SD. In contrast to the hands-on, firefighting activities typically performed, senior managers who lead product development take action to link planning and execution.

• *Team Launcher.* In this role, senior managers develop and/or approve charters for individual projects that have been designed to realize specific objectives established by the product line architecture and the business strategy. These charters set out the project's business purpose and provide the framework within which the project team will operate. In addition, senior managers select the people who will form the *core team* of the project: those who will be responsible for its execution. This charter development/team selection activity connects the foundation laying work on the left side of the drawing to the project execution work on the right.

• *Energy Source.* As the portfolio manager, senior management is charged with building the skills and capabilities—the organizational energy—needed for successful development. As the "energy source" on the back end, however, senior management must ensure that individual project teams get what they need to be effective. For some things, the team will be self-sufficient. But for many activities (e.g., building prototypes, market research, testing), the team will need support from the functional groups. Senior management's role here is to ensure that the functions provide excellent service to the team.

• *Commitment Manager.* Part of the senior manager's role in leading product development is periodically reviewing and examining the progress of individual projects in light of plans, commitments, and objectives at the level of the project, the aggregate project, and the business-as-enterprise. However, this is more than tracking dates and budgets. It is influencing, guiding, facilitating, and reviewing commitments.

As projects go forward, the nature of the commitments connected to their progress usually changes. Most efforts move from an early stage in which relatively little expense and commitment are involved, options are open, and many possibilities are considered, to later stages in which specific actions must be taken involving significant commitments. These include capital investments in new equipment or facilities and the determination of specific performance parameters, design elements, and other product features, all of which establish the identity of both the product and the product line—and of the business itself. In their role as "commitment manager," senior managers are responsible for ensuring that the commitments made are consistent with the financial abilities of the enterprise, its short- and long-term objectives, and its strategic position in the market.

• *Sponsor/Coach.* Once the purposes and boundaries of projects have been established and the effort launched, teams will continue to need help from senior management to guide their work. Senior managers thus play a critical supportive role as sponsor/coach, giving the team the necessary direction and guidance to interpret events, deal with unexpected contingencies, and otherwise negotiate the relationship between the individual project and the total set of activities within the portfolio and within the business. Being a sponsor, however, does not mean directing the project itself. The emphasis is on support and coaching.

• *Process Improver.* As owners/creators of the development process, senior managers are also responsible for its improvement. With their range of roles in new product development and their other executive responsibilities, senior managers are uniquely positioned to see the product development process in its entirety and to link all its different aspects to each other, to the business, and to the other processes and activities of the organization. As they do so, they are also uniquely positioned to isolate areas that need improving, to ensure that such improvement is made, and to make certain that what is learned on one project is transferred to others.

Product development led by senior management looks very different from product development that is not. Senior managers that take on the new roles we have laid out here build connections between the business strategy and the set of development projects the organization undertakes. They focus both on doing the right things and on doing things the right way. They are, in fact, building and executing a development strategy—the processes, activities, and capabilities that create the future of the enterprise.

When product development is led, the center of gravity in the enterprise shifts. Senior managers see the whole and actively create a portfolio of projects that collectively advance the business. Senior managers think of development strategy as creating the future for the business, which a *set of projects* then delivers. Projects are treated not as exceptions to normal systems, but as a natural way to take action.

The Board and Leading Product Development

Much of the attention of the Board of Directors focuses on two key questions: What are the realities of the company's current competitive and market positions and what near term performance results can be expected as a result? What are the prospects for the company's long-term success and what can be done in the near term to put the firm in a better position to capture those future opportunities? In addressing these questions, knowledge of the firm's product development capabilities and plans can be invaluable to the Board. In addition, the Board can provide much-needed perspective and input to senior management that will reinforce and improve ongoing development efforts.

Product development leaders—in this case, the CEO and perhaps the executive staff—encourage their boards to make product development central to their thinking. For example, as the Board reviews, discusses, and makes recommendations concerning the current health of the business, knowledge and information on product development realities can provide an important indicator of the fundamental needs and opportunities facing management. In addition, when product development is central to management's view of the business, by necessity, it must be central to the Board's compensation and performance evaluation discussions.

Similarly, as the Board interacts with senior management in evaluating the best long-term use of the firm's resources, looks for ways to strengthen and enhance distinctive capabilities and sustainable advantage, and motivates corporate actions, product development can and should play a central role. Because the firm's competitive and market positions in coming years will be determined largely by the products and services it offers—most of which will result from current or planned development efforts—regular, up-to-date reviews and discussions of product development strategies, development processes, and their performance results not only enable the Board to carry out its prescribed responsibilities, but to do so in a manner that is extremely valuable to senior management.

In a handful of firms we know firsthand, in which senior management effectively leads product development, we have observed significant and meaningful Board involvement in development along the following lines:

- In its annual review of the firm's strategies and approval of the coming year's operating plan, the Board includes a thorough review of the product development strategy, its primary goals, the projects planned for this year, and anticipated market introductions and results.

- The Board reviews and approves all major commitments of development resources, with special attention paid to plans that represent new directions for the firm's development efforts and to significant increases in levels of spending on development (such as creating and staffing an additional development team).

- The operating review section of each regular Board meeting includes a review of all major development projects, their anticipated results when initially approved, and management's current assessment of anticipated results.

It should be noted that the latter two activities are completely analogous to what most Boards do in connection with all major capital investments—the Board approves overall capital spending plans and major individual projects. Because product development commitments often can have an impact comparable to that of capital spending, equivalent processes for Board involvement are warranted.

- In its periodic review of competitors and the firm's competitive position—often done as part of the strategy review—the Board examines and discusses the strengths and weaknesses of the new product efforts of competitors. This gives added perspective and information when considering the firm's own plans regarding product line breadth and positioning, customer segment and channel evolution, longer-term technology thrusts, and planned resource allocations.

- As the Board reviews compensation programs and their links with performance results, new product development goals and achievements are considered as a fundamental management responsibility. In addition, the Board works with senior management to identify, recognize, and reward outstanding individual, team, and support staff contributions to the firm's development efforts.

While each of these approaches can be used with the entire Board of Directors, special committees of the Board—such as the Compensation Committee or the Technology Committee—can also focus on reinforcing the firm's development efforts. These contributions can involve even more depth and interaction with senior management, and ensure that long-term philosophies and policies—such as those associated with compensation structures and technology investments—are complementary and consistently applied.

From our vantage point, an excellent test of senior management's true beliefs regarding the importance and impact of product development in the firm's success is the extent to which the Board of Directors is knowledgeable about and involved in discussions of development activities. Senior managers who consider leading product development to be worthy of a major portion of their time and energy could not imagine their Board not having similar feelings. Nor would they want to pursue such a significant dimension of success on their own, without the benefit and reinforcement of the Board's direct involvement and contribution.

Above all, leaders of product development lead through substantive influence, and they exercise that influence at the right time. Fighting fires at the last minute, à la Joe Perina, is not exercising influence at the right time; indeed, it doesn't have a substantive influence at all: it only solves an immediate problem. And worse, it may encourage a recurrence of the problem, since it demonstrates that someone inevitably comes in and saves the day.

During a particular project's development, senior managers who lead product development see themselves as an energy source and as counselors. Because there is a development strategy in place, because senior management monitors projects in the aggregate, and because the individual project makes sense, these leaders are rarely called upon to pull irons from the fire. Rather, they are in the service business, providing resources, technology, skill, and capability when and where the teams need it. On the other hand, their business is coaching and counseling, providing the team and the team leader with a sounding board, encouragement, advice, and wisdom.

Then, as the individual project ends, senior managers who lead product development become involved in post-project audits, review programs, and the like, asking themselves, "What have we learned in this project? What went wrong? How can we make things better? *What went right?* How can that be integrated elsewhere? How can our development process be improved?"

Effective leaders lead by example. They send signals, through their allocation of time and attention, about what counts in the organization. By setting the agenda, they signal what is the business' focal point: where the center of gravity lies. Leaders establish the priorities and the high-leverage points, how much time and resources will be devoted to them, how they will be measured to determine success or failure. But in leading product development, senior managers must also take action. Theirs is a unique vantage point and a unique point of leverage. If they do not set direction, "architect" the product line, manage the project portfolio, create and improve processes, launch projects, coach and sponsor teams, supply energy, and manage commitments, those things will not get done. No one else sees the whole; no one else can shape it. But if they take on these roles, if they take action from their unique position, they can harness the energy and creativity in the organization to build the enterprise. This is what it means to lead product development.

3

Less Is More: Building an Effective Project Portfolio

In the front end of product development, where the business decides what ideas to pursue as development projects, how many projects to attempt, and how those projects fit with the business strategy, senior management's job is leadership. Leading product development at this stage means linking the business strategy to the set of projects the business plans to complete. Forging that link means taking action to ensure that the business gets the best ideas into the best projects, that the project portfolio realizes the strategy, and that the resources and capabilities deliver on the promises of the projects.

In Chapter 2 we identified four roles that senior managers play in carrying out this work. Here we look at each of the roles in some detail. The questions we address are: What is involved in carrying out the role? What should senior managers actually do? For each role, what tools, processes, and frameworks can senior management use to take effective action?

Leading Product Development

Below we examine the roles senior management plays in the front end and briefly lay out corresponding tools and mechanisms for playing those roles. We then discuss how senior management creates a coherent pattern of leadership by integrating the roles it plays and the tools it uses to play them.

Four Roles for Senior Management

Direction Setter

Senior management's role in setting direction for product development grows naturally out of its responsibility for overall business strategy. But setting a direction for product development is more than laying out a business plan. Senior managers need to take steps to make the strategy specific and concrete in its implications for product development. They need to set goals for the firm's development activities that will motivate action, guide decision making, and indicate what behaviors should be rewarded. Additionally, that direction must link product development to technology strategy and product/market strategy. In short, the key task is to define and communicate what product development must contribute for the business strategy to succeed.

Senior managers must articulate for the entire organization the direction they envision for product development (so that everyone understands where the set of activities leads), the performance impact expected, and how to recognize and track progress. Consider, for example, the challenge facing senior management at Old Line Inc., a (composite) consumer products company with several brands that are respected but have high costs and limited distribution. After losing share consistently for three years, the Board installed a new cadre of senior managers who set a new course for the business: break out of the old rut with lower-cost products that utilize the company's industry-leading technologies and build on the established brands, but take Old Line into new categories, segments, and channels. The goal was to do this without investing additional capital, and to do it over a much shorter period of time than had been the case in recent years.

In its role as direction setter, Old Line's senior management identified the key issues of performance for product development:

- Create base products (or "platforms") that can achieve a competitive advantage in the marketplace and that the business can leverage into multiple new channels and subsegments.
- Working with suppliers and operations, utilize new product development to effect a 30% reduction in product cost over the next two years.
- Expand the range of technologies embedded in the company's products.
- Seek out new segments in established categories with much lower-cost derivative products (increase market share by 5 points).
- Enter two new categories (i.e., add two new product lines) over the next three years.
- Be much more responsive; time to market on major products must be less than 18 months and on derivative products must be well under six months.
- Develop the capability to design products for a worldwide launch.

These critical tasks and objectives define neither specific projects nor specific products for development (although they do establish clear measurements of achievement). Instead, they lay out a strategic direction and clarify where attention and resources must be applied; in this sense, senior management is building an agenda for action throughout the business. When such direction is linked to the selection of projects to be pursued and made a topic of discussions, review, and planning at executive staff meetings and in performance evaluations, such direction setting guides day-to-day action and creates a new reality.

Leading Product Development

Product Line Architect

As in any journey, knowing the objective and having a clear direction is a useful starting point. But in product development, much more than direction is needed to establish strong connections between the business strategy and specific development projects. Essential to forging those links is action taken by senior management to define a framework for understanding the line of products the business offers today and plans to offer in the future. We call this framework the "product line architecture," and assign to senior management the role of "product line architect." This framework also complements, strengthens, and helps implement the role of direction setter.

From the vantage point of senior management, successful execution of the business strategy hinges on consistency in developing a series of excellent new products over time that meet the needs of target segments and deliver the intended breadth of price and performance to the market. Customers, of course, want individual products that address their current and future needs, will not soon be obsolete, are delivered on time, and meet their expectations of quality, functionality, and other performance dimensions. But customers also care about the product line: not only may they buy several offerings, but the character of the line affects brand identity, image, and the investments customers must make in using the products. Moreover, the nature of the product line—with its number of families, range of offerings, and frequency of improvements and changes—critically affects the operating cost structure involved in producing and delivering the products and the asset base of the business. How the line is structured and developed determines such things as manufacturability (and thereby cost and quality), material requirements, process reliability and flexibility, capital intensity, and asset utilization.

The challenge for senior management, therefore, is to "architect" the product line so that it covers the intended market in a manner distinctive from that of its competitors and highly valued by customers, while leveraging both development and operating resources. Because of the impact and importance of such architecting and the fact that it requires a broad, integrated perspective on customers, competitors, technology, and the firm's capabilities and strategies, it is fundamentally a senior management role. Furthermore, the opportunity for doing this is greatest at the front end, in advance of development efforts, with development projects then providing the means to implement product plans, turning them into products and services that can be delivered to customers with great success.

To carry out its role as product line architect, senior management needs to identify and evaluate alternative product line structures, craft an architecture that achieves strategic objectives, and communicate that framework to the organization. To make that mission concrete, we have found it useful to divide "architecting" into two parts. In the first, senior management defines the types of products in the line. This becomes a language for communicating choices about the structure of the product line and for defining the mission of individual products. In the second, senior management defines the relationship of the individual products in the product line and how the line will evolve over time. At stake here are the timing and frequency of product introductions, the sequencing of different elements in the lineup, and the pattern of benefits the product line brings to the market and to the firm.

DEFINING PRODUCT TYPES A useful way to distinguish among product types is to think in terms of the *change* the product introduces relative to current offerings. For senior management, the challenge is to find those dimensions of change that are most important for the business and then use them to calibrate the amount of change a given kind of product brings to the business. This process of calibration and classification usually leads to four broad types of products (and related production processes) whose specific definition will differ by business:

• *Breakthrough* products, as the name implies, depart significantly and fundamentally from existing practice. They may introduce highly innovative product or process technology, open up a new market segment, or take the business into a totally new arena.

• *Platform* products form the base of a product "family" that can be leveraged over several years and often across multiple market segments. Though not as radically different as a breakthrough, a new platform usually provides a substantial boost in value to customers and to the firm's competitive position. Thus, it may enable the business to address a new distribution channel or may involve a new manufacturing process.

• *Derivative* products are derived from other products—usually platforms. They may offer lower cost, enhanced features, or modifications in packaging. They usually extend the product line, fill in gaps in the offerings, exploit a niche, or otherwise leverage investments in a platform.

• *Support* products lie at the very end of the change spectrum, and entail only minor changes in technology, marketing, or processing to support the product line. These minor modifications support the product line by extending the range of its application, correcting a problem in an existing product, keeping it fresh in customers' minds, giving the sales force something "new" to discuss during regular customer visits, or customizing it for a specific customer.

The value of product change maps and product types lies in their use as a language for analysis and evaluation. Creating an architecture means looking at the mix and sequence of product types, and making judgments about the cost, impact, and value of alternative configurations. Defining product types in this way gives senior management the ability to look at choices from the standpoint of the business and its strategy. Specialists in marketing and product planning may need to do their work in the detailed language of specifications and formulations, feature sets, and psychographic profiles. But for architecture, senior management needs to think and talk about the product line in ways that communicate the role and impact of different elements of the line in the business.

"ARCHITECTING" THE PRODUCT LINE   The architecture of the product line reflects what the business is doing today and what it plans to do tomorrow. If senior management "freeze-frames" the products currently being offered, it has a picture of what they look like to today's customers. If it freeze-frames the current line plus the products under development, it gets a picture of how that product line will change in the near future. If it freeze-frames the planned set of new products, senior management creates the longer-term view. The product line architecture is a collection of these three frames of reference. To create the architecture, therefore, senior managers must project the business into the future, stop at the planning horizon and look back and ask, "What do we want the product line to look like, and how do we want it to evolve?"

An excellent tool for answering these questions and then capturing and sharing the product line architecture with others is the product generation map. As shown in Figure 3–1 for the Apple Macintosh product line during the latter half of the 1980s, this map conveys the relationships among breakthroughs, platforms, and derivatives. It indicates the lineage of various generations of product, locates them in terms of their price and performance, and identifies the timing of introductions.

Leading Product Development

Figure 3–1
MacIntosh/Lisa Product Line

Product Family

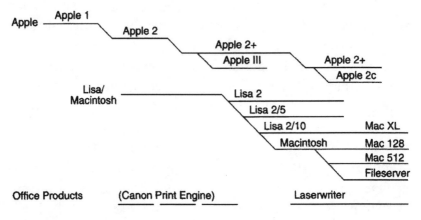

The Macintosh map deals with actual products. Projecting that map into the future does not require specifying in detail the concepts, features, and content of future products—such work is the job of the project teams. What senior management must do is lay out the product line's evolution in terms of product types, their relationship to current and future offerings, and the timing of their introduction. Moreover, they must do so in a way that fits the marketplace, the competitive environment, and the firm's resource realities. Four issues must be addressed to extend the map into the future and create the best product line architecture for the business:

- *Position.* Where in the lineup and in the price/performance set does the business and its strategy need new products? Answering this question focuses senior management attention on opportunities in the market, possible competitive moves, gaps in the lineup, and the breadth of line needed to accomplish the business objectives.

- *Type.* What kind of products will be most effective in meeting specific market needs? The choice of breakthrough, platform, derivative, or support has important consequences for the economics of the business and its ability to respond to contingencies.

- *Timing.* When should new products be introduced? The pace of technological change, price/performance economics, and market rhythms, as well as the ability of customers to make the transition from the old to the new and of the business to fund development at a sustainable pace, all must be factored into such timing deliberations. The time between the introduction of platforms in a given segment is critical, but the timing of derivatives (in a cluster? spread out over time?) has financial and market perception implications as well.

- *Relationships.* How will the new products be related? A key issue here is which derivatives will come from which platforms, but it is also important to establish the shared characteristics across platforms that define product line identity.

Architecting the product line requires that senior management make the business strategy come alive in specific products introduced at specific times, with specific roles in the line and specific relationships to other entries. Doing this work requires a good deal of information and insight into technology, markets, and competitors. It may be that one member of senior management—the head of marketing, for example—will direct the effort. But laying out the architecture, agreeing on its rationale and logic, and aligning efforts to make it a reality are so fundamental to the business and the work of every function that it must be accomplished by senior management working as a team.

The Importance of Platform Projects

Platform projects represent changes in both the product and, typically, how it is manufactured. Platforms combine a set of improvements and innovative ideas into a "system solution" for a broad range of core customer needs, and the majority of customers should perceive the new platform product as significantly better than either the prior platform or its derivatives. At the same time, platform products should be sequenced in ways that enable customers (and the business) to move from the previous generation to the new one. Generally, such platform development efforts appear to start with a "clean sheet of paper" and result in 80% or more of the product (and often the process) being redesigned. But ensuring customer acceptance and migration are key, which means that even new platforms must be compatible and provide continuity with prior offerings, as well as with subsequent new products. Hence, platform projects tend to require much more creativity and insight, and therefore resources, than do derivative efforts.

A classic example of a platform product is the Macintosh computer, built to form the core of a new product family based on Apple's highly successful Apple line (particularly the Apple II) and its breakthrough (albeit ill-conceived) Lisa line. The Mac was not only to be a product exhibiting new technology, it was to be manufactured in a very different way, in an automated factory. After many well-publicized, dramatic ups and downs necessitating modifications in the platform design following its initial introduction, the Mac finally hit its stride, moving from the Mac XL in 1985 to the next-generation platform encompassing the Quadra and Centris series in the early 1990s. Over the years, the Mac family increased its compatibility with IBM PC-type computers and software, greatly expanded the kinds of applications it could run, entered new distribution channels, yet maintained and refined its unique "look and feel." In 1994, the Power Macintosh platform, fueled by the PowerPC 601 microprocessor (developed in collaboration with IBM and Motorola), was introduced. Significantly, Apple's advertising for the Power Macintosh read, "This isn't just a new family of Macintosh personal computers. It's a whole new kind of personal computer." This, then, became the latest platform in a sequence of Macintosh generations.

Platform projects offer significant competitive leverage when done right. They can be leveraged into an entire family of products and be viable in the marketplace for several years. Moreover, the way they are structured sets out a road map of future projects and resource allocations and actualizes the evolving product line architecture. For example, if the platform is introduced as a fully featured offering that later will "spin off" stripped-down and cost-reduced versions, that decision goes a long way towards determining what projects the firm will want to initiate in the future, how they will be focused, and what resources they will require. A decision to introduce a bare-bones platform offering, adding features and options down the road, influences subsequent development projects just as critically. Thus, choosing the core offering's "center of gravity" and the number and variety of derivatives is one way senior management can provide significant influence and leadership.

Software development (e.g., WordPerfect 5.0 or Windows 3.0) also offers clear examples of platform projects and their power. Generally, the company begins with an X.0 identification code, signifying the platform and its version; subsequent offerings (either derivatives or enhancements) then are given codes like X.1 and X.2. Thus, through the product name, the company is signaling to the customer that the product line architecture is "X" and that the particular product is one or another version of it. Of course, some of those derivatives may be upgraded or error-corrected versions that replace a prior offering, rather than being "new" in the sense of added features or capabilities. However, even those projects can be related to a platform and its family of extensions.

Platforms can be found in the soft drink business as well. For decades, Coke and the Coke brand name represented a single platform. Then Diet Coke was introduced, which represented a "half platform," in a sense; it was clearly a different formula but it leveraged off the same advertising and brand identification. Then the company introduced—with vast fanfare—a new formula for Coke, which, so the company thought, would be a new platform, or new-generation offering. When a major segment of the market indicated that it still wanted the old platform, the company brought back Coke Classic, the original formula, while keeping the new Coke. From a market leverage point of view, the company has a single brand platform (Coke) that now comes in multiple formulas and variations—new Coke, Coke Classic, Diet Coke, caffeine-free Coke, and caffeine-free Diet Coke.

Perhaps the most significant benefit of having a product line architecture defined by senior management is that it provides a context and a set of boundaries for individual development projects.

Senior management no longer has to commit itself to projects based on single proposals that appear more or less randomly. It can shape and influence the development of proposals and the generation of ideas through the architecture it plans and develops. Furthermore, it can avoid the temptation to inject projects into the pipeline as a reaction to a specific, near-term pressure. The architecture establishes a set of expectations and a framework for matching development resources with projects to ensure that the highest leverage efforts get the needed resources. It is a critical link between the business strategy and the creation of an effective set of development projects—the project portfolio—that will bring the strategy to fruition.

Portfolio Manager

A product line architecture encourages senior management to think in terms of a *portfolio of projects,* in which individual projects represent deliberate efforts based on an assessment of what the organization (and its customers) wants the product line to look like in the future and what *portfolio of development capabilities* the business has to execute projects. As the portfolio manager, senior management must match up product line goals with new ideas, fold those ideas into specific projects, and match projects with development capability. Such capability involves both the aggregate capacity to do projects and the mix of development skills (software, hardware, test, prototype, and so forth).

All but the very smallest of firms have a portfolio of development projects—that is, they have multiple development projects going on concurrently—requiring the input of multiple skills and resources. Senior management, however, often thinks about the project set as the "current project list"—projects that have been approved and started, but not yet completed (or killed). While senior management adds projects to that list and periodically reviews important projects on it, it generally fails to manage the entire set as a portfolio, to balance it with the available capabilities and their capacity, and to manage development resources as a portfolio. As a result, there are too many projects by a factor of two or three, shifting resources move endlessly from one project to another, and everyone knows projects will be late—there simply aren't enough resources to get them done on schedule. Furthermore, because of insufficient resources, the best development people find themselves assigned to four, five, or even more projects concurrently. This spreads them so thin that their productive development time actually declines (they spend more time in "update meetings" and other nonvalue-added activities), further aggravating the problem of overcommitted resources.

The aggregate project plan (APP) is a powerful mechanism for managing the project portfolio and matching it with the capabilities portfolio. But like the product line architecture, the APP looks at the future as well as the present. It comprehends projects under development as well as projects yet to be launched, and current as well as future capabilities. Senior management has two tasks in putting together the APP: defining the project set, and matching projects with capabilities and their capacity.

• *Defining the project set.* The product line architecture sets out the desired evolution of the product line. Given project lead times, it defines the sequence of projects required to realize the plan. But it does not identify the specific content of the projects; that is a task for the APP. For senior management, putting the right projects in place involves a combination of "bottom up" and "top down" action. Project proposals will come in from many different sources. The challenge is both to select product ideas from those proposed, and to shape and influence the development and collection of ideas into projects. The result will be to define a sequence of projects, some of which will be done now (or are already under way), some of which will be done soon, and some of which will be done down the road. With a clear product line architecture, it is much easier to guide and direct the organization toward projects that fit the business strategy and implement development goals and objectives.

• *Matching projects to capability and capacity.* A project imposes requirements on the business. As portfolio manager, it is senior management's job to match requirements and capacity. Requirements differ by type of project and pertain to all of the resources needed to take an idea to market. Capacity is likewise comprehensive. What is at stake here is not just the sheer number of engineers or marketers, but the capacity for action. In addition to making sure that the numbers match, senior management must ensure that the business has the right set of skills, tools, and methods to carry out the project plan. The matching process requires that senior management build a base of information so it can estimate what is necessary to conduct a project of a certain type and thus determine the impact of individual projects on available capacity. But the most critical element in senior management's role here is discipline—to focus resources and to limit the number of projects under development to the capacity available to execute them. Our emphasis on discipline in the APP is based on the notion that less is more—putting *less* at a time into development avoids overloading, confusion, and congestion and results in *more* getting out.

When development capacity is overcommitted, as our studies suggest it normally is, senior management has failed to execute its leadership role. In essence, senior management is avoiding responsibility for making tough choices in advance, hoping that it will subsequently become obvious which projects deserve priority. But this has at least four negative consequences:

- Target dates do not become commitments because everyone knows priorities will shift and dates will be revised; almost all projects have longer cycle times (and cost more) as a result.
- Scarce resources are applied to projects that are given reduced priority and may never be (or hindsight reveals should not have been) introduced because they are no longer timely; that is, scarce resources are misused or not used optimally.
- Development productivity declines as projects ebb and flow and resources shift across projects, seldom providing the critical mass and focus needed to do things completely and correctly the first time.
- Because projects are not "naturally" on time and on target, under conditions of overcommitment, senior management guarantees that its intervention will be required at the eleventh hour.

By failing to make tough choices at the outset and letting far too many projects get (and stay) on the active list, senior management ensures the perpetuation of traditional behaviors in the organization.

The two senior management tasks we recommend clearly interact. Senior management shapes the project portfolio with capacity in mind; it builds capability and capacity in light of the architecture and project opportunities. Moreover, this is not a once and for all experience. The APP must be revisited, revised, and its time horizon extended on a regular basis. It is a rolling plan whose elements change and evolve as better information develops, projects get completed, and capacity to take on additional projects becomes available or is created. The rolling nature of the plan highlights two groups within the APP: 1) projects defined, approved, chartered, staffed, and launched; and 2) potential projects, consistent with the architecture but less well specified, and not yet staffed and launched. As senior management revisits the APP it may occasionally change something in the first group (e.g., kill or delay a project in trouble), but most changes to the APP will occur in the second group.

The result of this iterative process is a "living" plan and process. One way to communicate the plan is to graph the projects as time lines with start and launch dates, tied to particular product categories and matched against capacity. Figure 3–2 illustrates such a tool. Framed in these terms, the APP provides another context for senior management leadership. It is both a way to gauge progress and to plan for the future. As a single "snapshot," the APP shows the entire set of projects under way—from projects out on the horizon to those in development and almost ready for market introduction. At regular intervals (e.g., every quarter), senior management literally freezes the action to see what is going on: how the plan is evolving, how resources are being consumed, and what problems may be arising. At the same time, since it is consulted on a regular basis, the APP allows senior managers to see how these efforts will evolve and have evolved over time. Each APP snapshot, in effect, becomes a frame of a motion picture from which new lessons can be learned and appropriate actions can be taken.

The APP helps senior managers answer three questions critical in leading product development: *What is the right portfolio of projects, given our product line architecture? What is our capacity to execute development projects? Does the portfolio we envision match the capacity we have?* Clearly, finding the answers to these questions requires balancing the opportunity expressed in the architecture with the reality of getting projects to market. The APP and the architecture, therefore, must work in tandem.

Making senior management both the architect and the portfolio manager links the two processes. While the APP determines final resource commitments to particular projects, senior managers, when they make the first pass at resource commitment, develop and refine the future product line architecture. With its knowl-

Leading Product Development

Figure 3–2
Pre-Quip Time Line

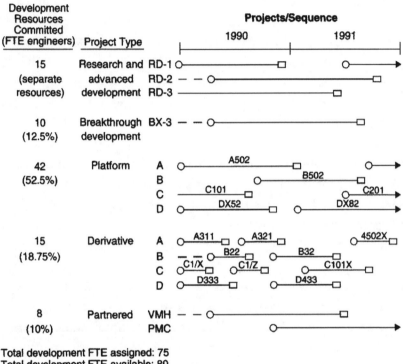

Development Resources Committed (FTE engineers)	Project Type		Projects/Sequence

Total development FTE assigned: 75
Total development FTE available: 80

edge of the APP, senior management can create a product line plan that recognizes not only what the market requires, but also the development capacity of the business. It does not at that point, however, finally commit resources to particular projects. That is what happens with the APP. With experience, these mechanisms shift the capacity allocation debate from the question, "Can't we just take on one more project, since we're overcommitted anyway?" to "What ideas and concepts need to go into a specific project so it achieves its business purpose?" Over time, senior management can also work to build the portfolio of development capabilities by removing bottlenecks, improving productivity, and adding new skills and resources as the value of doing so becomes clear.

Process Creator: Moving Ideas to Products through the Development Funnel

Working in tandem, the product line architecture and the APP give senior managers the tools to link ideas to projects, projects to products, and products to the business strategy. But for those tools to be effective in practice, they must be applied in the right sequence, at the right time, and in the right way. What senior management needs, in effect, is a *process* for applying the architecture and managing the project portfolio—a process senior management needs to create. In their role as process creators, senior managers are responsible for ensuring an ample flow of innovative ideas (as well as their validation prior to inclusion in commercial projects), creating a sequence of activities to turn ideas into projects that implement the product line plan, and defining milestones and decision points as products take shape so they enter the market as planned and have their desired impact.

The mechanism we suggest to tackle this role is the development funnel. The funnel depicts a process in which the organization, led by senior management, generates a large number of ideas, screens them to find those with merit, organizes good ideas into potential projects, takes the best of the projects to build the APP, launches them when their time comes, and reviews their progress toward market introduction. At various points in the process from the mouth to the narrow end, senior managers set up "screens" that serve as decision and review points, so that the right ideas become the substance of the right projects that deliver the right products.

Creating an effective funnel confronts senior management with four process imperatives. These imperatives define senior man-

Leading Product Development

agement's challenge and, at the same time, the value of the development funnel.

• *Creative ideas need to be encouraged and nurtured.* This has the effect of enlarging the open end of the funnel. Potential ideas can come from anywhere in an organization and from numerous sources beyond, such as customers, suppliers, competitors, and even academics. However, rarely do organizations have a systematic way of corralling these ideas. By and large, no one is responsible for their identification, no mechanisms are in place for their evaluation, no resources are available for further investigation, and many ideas simply wither from inattention. The point is to encourage creativity while also helping creative people see how their ideas could be translated into something of economic value.

• *Creative ideas need to be tested and evaluated.* Potential project ideas need to be tested and proven so that they are ready to be commercialized and far enough along to be folded into projects. This is an ongoing challenge for senior managers, since selecting the "right" new areas (with the right information, technology, markets, and so forth) is high risk. However, many of the mismatches that occur and are recognized when a product is introduced—for example, the customer says, "I don't want it," or a competitor has something better, or the technology is still unstable—can be traced back to not having the right ideas at the front end or failing to evaluate them (through an advanced development effort, if need be) prior to their inclusion in a development project. Senior management must evaluate ideas critically—not all deserve continuing consideration, and some should be killed.

• *Creative ideas need to be combined with other creative ideas to define effective projects.* All too often, a single creative idea—and particularly the creative *big* idea—forms the nucleus of a dedicated project. The result is a large number of projects, usually far more than senior managers are even aware of, some of which may be appropriate although many are not. Instead, the challenge is to merge several relevant creative ideas into a single project that makes sense strategically (i.e., in relation to product line architecture and the marketplace) and relative to what else is going on in product development (i.e., based on information drawn from the aggregate project plan).

• *Creative ideas need focused resources and staged commitments.* To become a product, creative ideas (packaged into an effective project) need resources applied effectively at the right time. If the mouth of the funnel is appropriately wide, there will be far more ideas than the business can possibly develop. The APP helps to focus resources, and the funnel needs to ensure that the development teams apply those resources effectively. Additionally, the commitments the business makes as ideas move toward the market need to be staged in order to manage the risks. Effectiveness means doing the right things right, and doing them at the right time.

The objective for senior management is to widen the funnel mouth by stimulating innovative ideas, to refine them to the point that they can be turned into appropriate commercial projects, and to focus resources on the critical few for development. This process of refining and focusing is what the screens in the development funnel are all about (see Figure 3–3 for an example). They define a set of milestones that give senior management a framework for making decisions and managing commitments.

Laying out a set of screens is the beginning of a funnel framework, but to make the funnel process work, process creators need to specify who is involved at the screens, how often screens occur, what criteria senior management will use in their evaluation, and what kind of work qualifies for review. The answers to these questions will differ depending on the nature of the market and the technical risks associated with new products, the pace of change,

Leading Product Development

Figure 3–3
Project Screens and Milestones

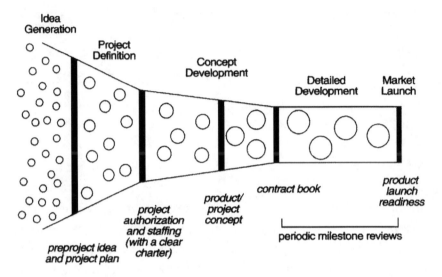

and the uncertainty confronting the business. The important point here is that senior management must recognize its role and address these questions in creating the process.

Once created, the process will only work if senior managers work it. As with the APP, the key to an effective development funnel is senior management discipline. If senior managers "inject" a special project into the funnel (thus bypassing the process), if they come in at a late stage and redirect the work, if they temporize and postpone action and delay decisions, or if they confuse the troops by waffling ("Did we pass that screen or didn't we?"), the process will break down. It will also break down if senior managers do not improve the process based on experience. This, too, is a matter of discipline, because it takes discipline to pay attention, review experience, and initiate effective change.

In a very real sense, senior management not only creates but also owns and operates the funnel process. It is theirs to make it work. Operated with discipline, the funnel can be a powerful integrating mechanism for managing the flow of ideas into products.

Developing a Development Funnel Process

One example of the effectiveness of a systematic effort to analyze the current development process and to rationalize screening criteria comes from Pilkington Barnes-Hind, PLC, a maker of contact lenses. Having already set to work developing an APP and architecting its product line, the organization now turned to establishing funnel screen criteria. (There is no universal approach to creating these three mechanisms; depending on the organization, its current development procedures, and myriad other factors, it is possible to set up these procedures in different ways and in different orders. Significantly, however, as PBH discovered, setting up an APP and determining a product line architecture are by themselves insufficient to create an effective development process. All three mechanisms must be integrated for a truly effective development process to take hold.)

Figure 3–4 shows the output of an off-site meeting of PBH senior managers in late 1993, wherein participants drew, and agreed upon, the current development funnel as they envisioned it. Because the firm had already initiated efforts to make the APP and the product line architecture part of its development process, the funnel depicted in the figure is not the twisted affair we sometimes see. What it did reveal, however, was how various crucial decisions were made very late in a typical project's day. At the #3 screen point, for example, is "financial targets/requirements." These should have been determined far earlier, when the project's charter and contract were being discussed. Similarly, "marketing/sales plans," also a #3 criterion, needed to be incorporated into the project contract. Moreover, having key marketing input at this very late point significantly increased the risk of snafus and delays. Even in #1, the "existence of internal champion" criterion suggests that a project needs particular support, rather than being considered only on its own merit, as part of a product line architecture requirement.

Figure 3–4

PBH's Development Funnel as Depicted by Senior Managers

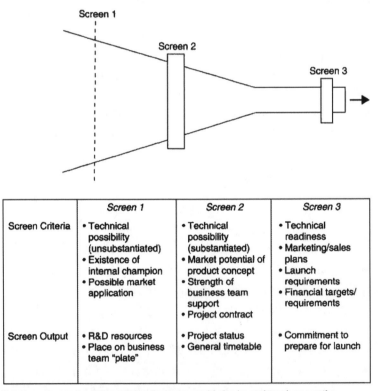

	Screen 1	Screen 2	Screen 3
Screen Criteria	• Technical possibility (unsubstantiated) • Existence of internal champion • Possible market application	• Technical possibility (substantiated) • Market potential of product concept • Strength of business team support • Project contract	• Technical readiness • Marketing/sales plans • Launch requirements • Financial targets/requirements
Screen Output	• R&D resources • Place on business team "plate"	• Project status • General timetable	• Commitment to prepare for launch

Between screens 2 and 3, project milestones would also be reviewed, as per the schedule agreed to during screen 2.

Thus, even in an organization where product development was significantly better than average, creating a development funnel was highly illuminating for senior management. At a minimum it revealed why project cycle time—getting to market on time— remained a problem for the company.

Putting It All Together

As tools of senior management, the power of the product line architecture, the APP, and the development funnel lies in their integration. The way we have defined it, the product line architecture is a road map for senior management as it sifts and shapes ideas into projects, matches them with capabilities and capacity, and creates the APP. The funnel is the process senior managers use to do the sifting and shaping. Framed in these terms, the architecture and development capacity are criteria (along with other things like technical feasibility and financial returns) for screening ideas and projects, and the project portfolio is an outcome of the funnel process that actualizes the planned product line architecture.

To work effectively as an integrated front-end process, the architecture, the APP, and the funnel must be coherent in content and timing. There are two broad ways for senior management to pursue this integration. In an architecture-driven approach, the product line architecture itself determines the timing and rhythm of screening decisions and the creation of the APP. In architecting the product line, senior managers attach a market window to projects and thus determine when the project should enter the APP and the development pipeline. For example, putting a platform product in the market in June 1997 might mean that the project must be authorized and in the APP by January 1996, which means there must be an architecture and a sifting and shaping of ideas

Leading Product Development

going on in mid- to late 1995. With this approach, senior management uses the architecture to screen ideas and projects. It rejects or saves for another day ideas that do not fit into the timing or the content of the architecture.

With an idea-driven approach—which fairly could be called "opportunistic"—the gestation of the ideas themselves establishes the rhythm of the screening process and drives decisions about whether a project will be created. In essence, there is no specific market window that determines when projects get created or whether a project will be approved. There is a broadly defined architecture for the product line, but the evolution of the ideas shapes the emerging architecture. This approach often characterizes businesses in very turbulent environments, where markets and technologies are extremely dynamic or where margins are high and opportunities rich. Some might argue, for example, that entire divisions in Hewlett-Packard's scientific instrument group have followed this strategy for decades—with notable and sustained success. Silicon Graphics, a successful player in high-performance engineering workstations and graphics systems, is another example of a company that has taken the idea-driven approach to front-end integration.

Most businesses will need to balance these two approaches to integration. Picking one or the other is not the point. What matters is recognizing the power of an architecture, an APP, and the funnel working in harmony, integrated in a way that works for the business. Where those three processes are in place, senior management has a way to effectively exercise leadership in the front end of product development. Where these processes work, product development is indeed at the heart of the business, and squarely on senior management's agenda. Without such a process, businesses end up with too many projects—and worse, far too many projects that are not strategically significant. This represents not only a financial drain but wasted opportunities. No organization can survive very long in today's unrelenting competitive arena with those twin millstones around its neck.

Consistently successful product development demands senior management's leadership. Senior managers are essential in crafting the framework of the three processes, integrating them, and making them fully effective through personal participation. This may require more time—significantly more time, in many cases—but that is precisely the point. Senior managers are bringing attention and influence to bear where they belong: at the front end of product development where they can see the parts and the whole.

Senior managers who become personally involved in leading product development do not see themselves as asset managers, moving resources around based on what someone else determines is the best opportunity. Instead, they themselves lead the process of determining opportunities (by being chief architects) and influencing key decisions (via the funnel process) based on a thorough understanding of resource and capacity issues (expressed in the APP).

Ultimately, by taking charge of the funnel, the architecture, and the APP, senior managers set the stage for successful projects before the curtain goes up and the execution of those projects begins. As we've noted, this is not a 100% guarantee that everything will turn to gold, but it sure beats the alternative.

4

Creating Consistently Effective Project Teams

Achieving consistent excellence in developing new products demands senior management leadership to build a solid foundation in strategy, planning, and capability. But at the end of the day, the ability to conceive, launch, and execute great projects that create distinctive products is also essential. Here, too, senior management leadership is crucial. By this we do not mean that senior managers should micromanage project execution or engage in the last-minute heroics that typify traditional product development approaches. Instead, just as successful, consistent development performance hinges on new mechanisms (i.e., the funnel, architecture, and aggregate project plan described in Chapter 3) and a new role for senior management in laying the foundation, it also entails a new approach to leading and executing projects, and a new role for senior management in making it work.

The challenge is classic: build creativity and depth of expertise in the disciplines and the functions, and develop processes to apply

Leading Product Development

and integrate that expertise to create great products consistently. Teams are an important part of the answer. Outstanding products need leadership and teamwork. They need project leaders and project teams that see the product as a whole, grasp the connections to the business, understand the parts, and effectively integrate them to achieve a coherent system that surprises and delights customers. Much of what we have to say about senior management leadership in project execution is about making teams work.

But teams do not exist in a vacuum; they need something to integrate. Great products spring from creative ideas in design and marketing, expertise in engineering and manufacturing, and outstanding logistics and distribution. Moreover, teams need the right kinds of people, information, and capital at the right times to apply those great ideas and that expertise to specific opportunities. In short, the disciplines, systems, and functions in the organization must provide the right supporting context if teams are to thrive and succeed. Senior management leadership is critical in providing, organizing, and marshaling that support.

In this chapter we will look at how teams and the functions that support them can be made to work effectively and consistently across many different kinds of projects and over time. There has been much discussion (to which we have contributed) in recent years of cross-functional integration, teams, and teamwork; what we emphasize here are the pivotal activities senior managers perform in ensuring that teams, in fact, work. These activities include:

- Defining project boundaries, missions, and charters.
- Picking the right kinds of teams (or, more precisely, matching the project type to the team type).
- Creating job opportunities and career paths that result in qualified team leaders and core team members, and that support individuals when, where, and in the quantities needed.
- Ensuring that functions build capabilities so that teams have the

right knowledge, tools, and other resources needed to achieve their objectives.

- Ensuring that the actions of teams are not only effective in achieving individual project goals, but also fit well with the overall strategy of the business and the evolution of its organizational capabilities and momentum.
- Supporting the team in dealing with unforeseen contingencies and the midcourse corrections required to keep the project on track and performing effectively.
- Ensuring that upon completion, there is a seamless transition of responsibility to the operating organization.

All these activities are essential to consistent product development success; they flow naturally from both the new roles of senior managers (described in Chapter 2) and the three foundation mechanisms—product line architecture, the aggregate project plan, and the funnel—explained in Chapter 3.

Before addressing teams and the new senior management role, we take a close look at the context in which teams operate. The starting point for our look at senior management and project execution is not the teams themselves, but the functions that support them.

Building the Stage 4 Enterprise

How the functions operate—and in particular, their strategic role in the business—has an important influence on how well they work in product development. In the business that fully capitalizes on the true power of teams, senior management pursues balanced excellence across the functions, and runs the business so that each function is a source of competitive advantage in more than its own "area" of responsibility. How a functional group participates in the business depends on the stage of evolution it has achieved in its strategic role.

Leading Product Development

Drawing on the framework developed by Hayes and Wheelwright (1985), we can distinguish four stages in that evolution:

Stage 1: Minimize Negative Potential—Be Internally Neutral.

Also known as "don't rock the boat" or "stay out of trouble," this stage puts the function in a narrow, operating role, with no influence on strategic decisions. Senior management recognizes that the function's work is necessary, but like its parking lots or the plumbing in its building, the function is not competitively important. The people running the function are not real "players" on the senior management team, and their career opportunities seldom extend beyond their function—in part because of their narrow, tactical role.

Stage 2: Match Competitors—Be Externally Neutral.

At this stage, the function has begun to focus on competitors and uses "normal" or "standard" industry practices to guide and gauge its performance. While the function provides more value to the business than it did in Stage 1, it has only a limited strategic role and is often expected to use outside help—consultants and senior management intervention—when it encounters strategic issues.

Stage 3: Back the Strategy—Be Internally Supportive.

Once the function has achieved Stage 3, it makes decisions in light of the business strategy and strives to provide credible support to key business objectives. The key strategic question for the function is, "What does this function have to do well in order for the business strategy to succeed?" The people running the function are on the senior management team, but they are not expected to shape the strategy. In this role, they are to do the best they can as a function without requiring significant changes on the part of others. Theirs is a progressive yet bounded and derived role.

Stage 4: Pursue a Distinctive, Sustainable Advantage—Be Externally Supportive.

A Stage 4 function is recognized and valued as a source of competitive advantage by customers and the other functions; its capabilities help distinguish the business from its rivals. Indeed, senior management, as a team of peers, shapes the business strategy in order to exploit the function's capabilities. The people running the function understand their strategic role, seek to identify longer-term trends and opportunities, and build capability in anticipation of strategic needs. Such capability does not remain solely within the function, however; it adds value to the work of others as well. The head of the function is a key player and peer on the senior management team.

Within a business, different functions may be at different stages of evolution. In the traditional high-tech enterprise, for example, it is not uncommon to find R&D pursuing Stage 4, while marketing and manufacturing are expected (and content) to perform at Stage 2. In such a situation, R&D drives the enterprise, holds the power in setting strategic direction, provides most of the career opportunities into senior management, and calls the shots in product development. In the consumer packaged goods industry, on the other hand, it would be more common to find marketing pursuing Stage 4 and wielding significant influence, with R&D and manufacturing (not to mention purchasing or human resources) at Stage 2, reacting to and following developments in the industry. In both of these cases (and others with an uneven pattern of evolution), product development mirrors the business: one function dominates the process and directs the effort, while the other functions react, come in late, and scramble to meet performance targets and deadlines.

Such a structure may work fine where competition is weak, time-to-market and project efficiency are not crucial, and customers are content with satisfactory products. But where competition is rigorous, cost and time critical, and customers demanding, such an uneven, unbalanced structure is ineffective and creates a significant competitive handicap. Even moving the lagging functions to Stage 3, while helpful, will not suffice. In that setup, the lagging functions still lack the stature and capability for effective integration.

The solution is a Stage 4 enterprise, where each function is a source of competitive advantage, the advantages created are complementary and reinforcing, and the heads of all the functions are key players on the senior management team. This last point is critical: the senior management team sets the tone and pattern for all the product development teams and supporting players. It defines what it means to work as a team of peers: with effective problem solving, with each function delivering excellence and advantage, and with team members working to contribute to the full potential of the function while maintaining the breadth and perspective needed to build the business. Moreover, the senior managers head up the functions. How they direct their functions has a crucial impact on the way team members who represent the functions and support activities within the functions carry out their work.

Thus, one of the most crucial actions senior management must take to achieve consistent excellence in product development is to upgrade the strategic role of the functions. This entails identifying the current stage of evolution for each function and laying out what needs to be done to move lagging functions to the next stage (and, ultimately, to Stage 4). A key first step in that process, and one consistent with the new front-end role for senior management laid out in Chapter 2, is to ensure that the heads of the functions are part of the senior management team—not just in name, but in practice. This in turn requires selecting, training, and developing managers whose skills, knowledge, expectations, and behaviors are "Stage 4."

The goal is to create a Stage 4 senior management team, even if the functions are not all there yet. Individuals at Stage 4 bring expertise and experience to the challenge of running the business. Stage 4 individuals are proactive in their approach, always looking for good ideas and better ways to do things in order to take the business forward. They are a great asset to the senior management team and an outstanding role model for the people in their functions.

Creating a Stage 4 senior management team is the crucial first step in building the Stage 4 enterprise. Many other things must be done to realize that goal, but getting the leadership team in place—with the right focus and a shared understanding of the path ahead—is the first step. It is also the first step in building the right context for teams and teamwork. In fact, pursuing teams in product development and pursuing the Stage 4 enterprise are mutually reinforcing: building the senior management team is the first step, but continuing on that path to make teams work in product development will help to move all the functions more solidly and aggressively toward Stage 4.

Making Teams Effective

For senior management, the challenge in project execution is to make teams work consistently and effectively in project after project. But projects differ from one another, and different types of projects require different types of teams. We have identified four principal team structures around which most development activity occurs; the key differences across these structures are the role of the team leader, the commitment of those doing the work, and who controls and allocates critical resources. Broadly, the four types span a continuum ranging from a purely functional structure to an independent team organization. We label these types functional, lightweight, heavyweight, and autonomous (see Figure 4–1).

Leading Product Development

Figure 4–1
Types of Development Teams

1: Functional Structure

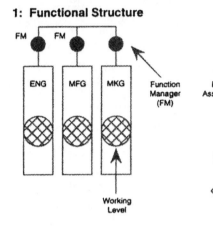

2: Lightweight Project Manager

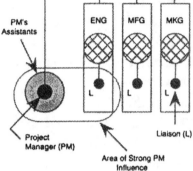

3: Heavyweight Project Manager

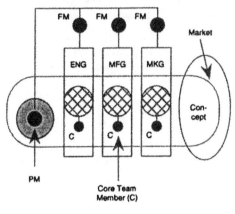

4: Autonomous Project Team

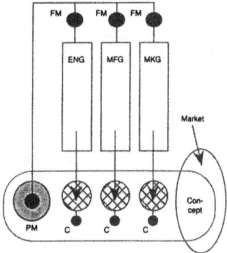

Functional teams, found most often in large, mature businesses, are, as their name suggests, organized by functions, with each team (or subteam) working under the direction of a specialized department manager (of manufacturing process engineering or software architecture design, for example) and a senior functional manager (e.g., of manufacturing or software). The work of these departments and functions is planned in advance through detailed specifications combined with occasional meetings to iron out issues that cut across disciplines. Each function, however, "owns" the work processes it uses, and seeks to apply them in a fairly uniform fashion, independent of the specific project and its nature. Responsibility for project work shifts over time from one function to the next according to prior agreement as to who controls what—a procedure that does not always run smoothly or quickly. The Global Electronics project described in Chapter 1 exhibited this structure as initially organized.

Lightweight teams are characterized by functional representatives—liaisons—who comprise a committee, directed (or, more descriptively, coordinated) by a lightweight project manager, that attempts to schedule, encourage, and track the project's various activities. The basic work and the bulk of the decision making take place back in the functions, and the functional representatives remain part of their disciplines, with the liaison role added to their regular responsibilities.

The lightweight manager, often a design engineer or product marketing manager (i.e., a middle- or junior-level person), is generally someone who has expertise in his or her function but no status or influence; this project assignment, then, is considered a way of broadening his or her experience in the larger organization. The "lightweight" designation also implies the manager's lack of control over resources (including people), which remain the responsibility of the functional areas. Thus, while lightweight managers coordinate project activities (e.g., by scheduling, expediting, and updating), and keep the relevant functions apprised of the work, they can neither reallocate resources nor reassign people within the project. Typically, these managers spend about 25% of their time in this role and describe their key activities in terms such as "reminding," "encouraging," "persuading," and "pleading."

Heavyweight teams give the heavyweight project leader responsibility for the total project effort and its overall success. This includes integrating functions and bringing the "voice" of the customer into the process. The heavyweight leader is often quite senior in the organization, and brings both expertise and organizational clout to the project. The heavyweight team itself consists of a core group of functional leaders responsible for work on the project and the majority of project decisions in their functions. While much of the work goes on in the functional groups, it goes on under the direction and influence of the heavyweight team and its leader.

Autonomous teams, or "tiger teams," are heavyweight teams whose members have been pulled out of the functions and transferred to the project. In their pure form, team members are co-located (as is usually the case with heavyweight teams) and self-contained. Leading the team is a heavyweight project leader—a general manager—who has full control over resources and exclusively evaluates team members' individual performance. Furthermore, the team and its leader have great latitude as to the choices they make, the processes they use, and the sources from which they seek support and assistance (usually outside the organization).

Each type of team has strengths and weaknesses (see Table 4–1). The functional team structure is well suited to advanced development projects, or to projects in stable environments where depth of knowledge and technical excellence are crucial. The development of an antistatic coating for microfilm at Kodak is a good example. Needing a new coating to reduce static, engineers at Kodak with long experience and a deep understanding of film and coatings were able to evaluate alternative technologies, spot a solution,

Table 4-1
Strengths and Weaknesses of Various Team Types

	Strengths	*Weaknesses*
Functional	Optimal use of resources, expertise, depth, scale economies; control and accountability; career path congruence	Lack of breadth; rigid, bureaucratic; task- not project-oriented; slow, disjointed; turf/expertise-driven
Lightweight	Improved communication and coordination; less idle time between tasks	Weak project leader and project focus; frustrating to individuals
Heavyweight	Strong project focus, commitment and accountability; integrated system solution	Hard to staff; requires breadth; must break down functional barriers
Autonomous	Focus on results; owns business objectives; innovative	Independent/not integrated with rest of organization; autonomy is core value

develop the rigorous protocols for production, and bring the product to market in 14 months.

When time and responsiveness are more critical and coordination is more valuable, but the predominant organizational structure is functional, lightweight teams are useful, particularly on derivative-type projects. These efforts address incremental product changes, with little or no process change. As such, they leverage existing products and may require substantially fewer resources than other types of projects. Having a coordinator (the lightweight project manager) who attends to the schedule and keeps communication flowing can be quite helpful in reducing lead time and improving productivity in most derivative products. Examples of such a project would include a different package for a cereal box or a new addition to a soup (say, broccoli added to an existing cheese soup).

As projects take on more complexity, uncertainty, and ambiguity, however, a "heavier" team structure is far more effective. Platform or next-generation projects, such as a new passenger car or a new family of computers, are most effectively executed with a dedicated core team and leader. This heavyweight structure gives the team the focus, leadership, and resources it needs to cope with turbulence in the environment. Yet, it allows the new product to fit well with the existing product lineup and operating system of the business.

However, when the challenge is to break entirely with the past, enter a new market, or do something radically different technically or commercially, the autonomous team is often most effective. Breakthrough projects are inherently nontraditional and lend themselves to the "clean sheet of paper" approach associated with autonomous teams. The team has the heavyweight leadership it needs, but autonomy frees the team from convention and gives it the ability to come up with invigorating changes that may spearhead a move into an entirely new area for the business.

Just as certain types of teams fit best with particular types of projects, each team requires different types of people. Part of senior management's leadership responsibility is to ensure that the necessary people are available in sufficient quantity to staff the projects. We mentioned earlier some of the differences in stature, decision-making authority, and integrative skills of the various team leaders. But similar differences are associated with the core team members. For functional teams, core team membership requires depth of expertise and mastery of the disciplines used within the function. On lightweight teams, it helps to have core team members with knowledge of the full breadth of their function (as opposed to only a few of the subfunctions). But since they are mainly liaisons, no decision-making authority is needed. Their job is more like a staff assignment.

In sharp contrast to the liaison position of lightweight core team members, heavyweight and autonomous team members hold a line position in the project. They must have both breadth and depth: breadth so they can help manage the entire project, address cross-functional opportunities, and recognize opportunities to add value to the work of others; depth so they can make judgment calls within their own function, commit their function on the range of project issues that arise, and direct the work of others within their function. Such core team members, who are still relatively junior in the organization, generally are in very short supply, especially in functionally structured firms. Creating career paths, developing breadth, and attracting people who get excited by such opportunities for early personal development are areas where senior management must take the lead.

While having the right kinds of people available and matching project and team types are necessary conditions for success, one other ingredient is also essential: having procedures, practices, and tools available that are well known by the organization and can be effectively leveraged by the teams and others on whom they will call for support. Again, senior management must set the agenda, focus the resources, and provide the direction so such processes become real assets and strengths, not random occurrences.

To meet the challenge of creating consistent, excellent project execution using different types of teams, senior management must play four specific roles: team launcher, energy source, commitment manager, and sponsor/coach. All of these are critical to organizing and leading project teams and require planning, attention, and action. Except for the sponsor role, the entire senior management team plays these roles as a unit.

Projects and Teams at Chaparral Steel

Chaparral Steel, a mini-mill located in Midlothian, Texas, produces well over a million tons of carbon-steel products a year and prides itself on its successful, continuing, and consistent ability to improve both its products and processes. The company establishes three types of projects: major advanced development, platform, and incremental. At any point, 40 to 50 projects may be under way: one or two of the advanced type, three to five platforms, and the remainder incremental. Significantly, each type has a different team organization.

Incremental projects (which require from a few $1000 to $200,000 in investment and last a few months) are almost all executed by functional departments with a lightweight project manager. At Chaparral, however, the lightweight project manager gets respect and cooperation: with so many projects under way, and with so many of them being incremental, just about everyone will be a lightweight manager sooner or later. Because so many know they will probably want the help of others at some point, they willingly give their own support when called on to do so.

Platform projects (from a few $100,000 to $1 million, and lasting anywhere from 12 to 24 months) are headed up by heavyweight project leaders. These team leaders usually are department managers, who, after their tenure as the head of a team, return to their (or other) departments. Under their guidance is a cross-functional team of five to seven members who both represent their function on the project and are jointly responsible for achieving success.

Finally, advanced development projects (with budgets of several million dollars and taking three to five years to complete) are directed by one of a small number of general foremen, who reports to a vice president (of manufacturing, for example). These projects often begin as advanced development efforts, but once technical feasibility is proven they become breakthrough efforts, with little or no change in team structure. Their charge is to complete products that offer substantial market opportunity *and* to develop the needed production processes.

For more than a decade, Chaparral has used this mixed approach to development projects and team structures in its highly competitive and volatile industry. Depending on the product or process challenge facing the company—the degree of technical complexity, innovation, task integration, and coordination required—it can pick the team type, the project leader, and the team members, all of which ensure that the effort will be successfully completed. Moreover, Chaparral is able to match the team type to the project type while also maintaining and strengthening a Stage 4 role for each of its functions. This has enabled the company to compile an outstanding record over the past two decades in an extremely competitive industry.

Carrying Out Senior Management's Roles

Team Launcher

Armed with a clear sense of business strategy, a process for generating ideas and deciding which should go into projects, a product line architecture, and an aggregate project plan, senior management is uniquely poised to launch individual projects. The launch is crucial. Unless the project and the team get off to a good start, it is difficult, maybe even impossible, to recapture lost ground. The Global Electronics case is again a prime example. And, as the Amalgamated Spectrometer Division vignette indicated in Chapter 2, while it is possible to pull off the last-ditch save, that is neither sustainable nor indicative of effective product development in the aggregate.

As team launcher, senior management has four key tasks, discussed below.

• *Establishing the Project Charter.* A project charter defines the business purpose of the project and establishes broad performance objectives. Such explicit, measurable, and briefly stated goals have power because they are connected to the strategy for the business. They help to bound the project, motivate the team, and guide its performance. As a focusing device, the charter is an early milestone in the development funnel and a key element of the team launch. It provides the anchor or foundation needed for the team to create and execute a detailed work plan successfully.

• *Matching Teams and Projects.* The charter defines the type of project. The next task is to match the team to the project. This entails matching project type and team type along the lines we discussed earlier. It also involves determining the makeup of the core team (including its size and the functions to be represented), the project leadership required, and the general scope of the team's initiative (which is also related to the type of project/team selected).

• *Selecting the Right People.* Senior management must exercise judgment and initiative in finding, selecting, hiring, and training the *specific* people who will fulfill a project's charter. At Toyota, for example, senior managers explicitly choose a project leader whose personality is consistent with the type of product they intend to introduce. Thus, when it was a sporty car targeted to a young, aggressive customer, they looked for a project leader who was a "fighter-pilot" type. When the project was to develop a luxurious sedan, they selected an executive type. The aim is to select project leaders who, by identifying with both the project and the customer, can internalize much of what counts in the product's total system performance.

Two other dimensions are especially critical when senior management chooses teams. One is the need for balance so that team members can function as peers. Imbalance among individual members (i.e., in their qualifications and effectiveness) invariably leads to imbalance and mismatch in the completed product. Second is the need for continuity in assignments so that individuals join a team with the expectation that they are there for the duration. Senior management must take the lead in establishing and supporting such discipline so that team leaders do not find themselves switching horses in midstream—having to bring someone new up to speed on the project and integrate him or her into the team's daily routine.

• *Executing the Contract Book.* With the project charter established and the core team and its leader selected, senior managers next turn to completing, in conjunction with the team, the project's contract book phase. This, in essence, entails preparing a statement of the relationship between the team and senior management—a joint commitment from both parties—with respect to the work plan and its deliverables. The team specifies how work on the project will be conducted, estimates the resources involved, and outlines the results on the basis of which it thinks its efforts should be evaluated. The contract book identifies to senior management what the team promises to deliver. Senior management, in turn, commits itself to providing the resources and support needed to achieve those objectives, as well as the appropriate recognition and rewards once they are. Generally, both the team members and the senior managers sign the book to indicate their agreement with and commitment to the project and its performance goals.

Charters and contract books are the primary formal mechanisms linking senior management and the team. When done effectively, they create an ongoing process that provides the right amount of guidance, interaction, and discipline. Getting the boundaries and the focal points just right is especially critical, for if senior managers are involved too much, in the wrong way, or at the wrong time, they will disempower the team; too little involvement or involvement of the wrong form creates the risk of a floundering team or senior managers who feel out of touch and respond by intervening unproductively.

The four activities—chartering the project, matching project and team types, selecting the right people, and drawing up the contract book—enable senior managers, as team launchers, to connect the front-end foundation to the specific project and product in a direct and concrete way.

Energy Source

Teams need resources, capability, services, and support to get the work done. Some of the "energy" to acquire, focus, and apply those critical inputs will come from the team, some will come through functional groups, and some will come from senior management. The amount and quality of what the team gets is determined in large part by senior management. Senior management is responsible not only for building the capabilities—in design, market research, testing, and manufacturing—that the team needs, but also for deploying those capabilities to specific tasks on specific projects. Senior management sets the tone and example for others to follow.

Energy, Projects, and Teams

Matching project types and team types raises two important and interrelated questions for senior managers wearing their "energy source" hats. The first is, if the plan calls for a certain kind of project, does the business have the type of team needed to execute it? If the plan includes several projects of the same type, does the business have sufficient energy— enough people, resources, and support—of the type that will be needed?

The second question is, does the business have the capability to marshal various types of teams? Functional and lightweight teams are roughly similar; businesses that are strongly functional in systems and practices will not have too much difficulty implementing the latter, which basically will only require overlaying a functional structure with a coordinating mechanism. Likewise, organizations that have adopted a team-oriented approach will not have much difficulty making the transition from heavyweight teams to autonomous ones, and back again.

Moving to the heavyweight form, however, can be problematic for the functionally oriented organization. Attempting to graft a heavyweight team onto a highly functional structure usually results in something like a "middleweight" team; to have truly heavyweight teams, the organization needs to institute significant and often dramatic changes. Making these changes—developing the energy to participate in heavyweight teams—is part of the energy source role of senior management. So too is getting others in the organization excited about possibilities, focusing creativity on how to make them happen, and then sustaining efforts when the unexpected occurs and the forces for the status quo appear too great to overcome.

Thus, the energy source role is particularly salient for the heads of functions. Compared to their traditional responsibilities in a function-centered system, the behavior of such senior functional managers must be quite different in the team-centered approach. The team has responsibility for the particular product going into the particular market. It makes the tradeoffs, selects the features, and seeks the coherence and functionality that will meet the specific mission laid out in the charter. As a source of energy, senior functional leaders in the team-based approach undertake actions to ensure that the project team receives timely support and service.

The service/support aspect is key. Senior managers who are functional heads face significant challenges in adopting the very different role that full participation in a business-focused product development process implies. For those who have been at Stage 2, the new role calls for getting ahead of the game—anticipating development needs and building the right capability to play the game from the very beginning. For those who viewed themselves as alone at Stage 4 and may have called the shots in the old days, the new role calls for moving away from the details of design and marketing so the team can have scope for action.

For this to work, senior managers have to get into the service business. They must learn how to work within a longer time horizon; they must understand how to succeed by developing functional capabilities, processes, and tools that can be parlayed by development teams. They must take pride in both creating this energy and delivering it to individual project teams without taking direct credit for project results. And at the same time, they must recognize that their own decision-making responsibilities are different.

This in no way implies a diminution of responsibility and influence; indeed, by ensuring consistently successful development performance through these mechanisms, they increase. Better yet, by rationalizing influence and attention, this approach magnifies the skills and experience that senior managers bring to bear on product development. They may no longer fight fires or design the graphics on the package, but they will have the satisfaction of seeing product after product hit the market with impact. This is a different way of doing business, and the energy source role underscores that fact.

Commitment Manager

Once a project has been chartered, the contract book approved, and the commitment to provide support and service to enact the project's goals made, the project team must deliver the agreed-upon results according to the timetable planned. As the team proceeds, however, it faces many options and uncertainties that need resolving. It also begins to accumulate information, the understanding of which will allow it to resolve these issues. As this happens, the team increasingly makes commitments that not only will influence the product's performance but also may affect customers' perceptions of the entire product line, as well as how the business' assets are being used. These commitments need to be managed, and senior management is in the best position to play that role.

For example, at Braun, a German consumer products company, a team developing a low-cost coffee maker faced a crucial choice: should it adopt a new, inexpensive material for the coffee-maker housing? The material would help the team meet its cost targets, but its appearance might conflict with Braun's image as a high-quality, high-value design producer. Because the low-cost version was to be sold under the Braun brand as part of the Braun line, the material choice would affect not only the product line but the entire company. The issue was critical to achieving Braun's growth and profitability objectives, and it demanded (and received) senior management attention. This was a commitment that needed to be made in light of the enterprise strategy. Happily, Braun's designers came up with a clever way to use the material while enhancing its aesthetic appeal. But senior management leadership was crucial in retaining commitment to the goal of the original charter while supporting the team in its responsibility to resolve the dilemma.

It is in the context of leadership that the commitment manager role comes to the fore. Beyond reviewing the extent to which a project is on track and meeting its objectives as defined in the contract book (i.e., reviewing the team's progress in delivering on its commitments), senior managers need to assess how these emerging commitments in the project stack up against the business strategy, commitments being made on other projects, and the relationship between the emerging project and the product line architecture. They need to ensure that the actions of the teams not only are effective in achieving the project's individual goals but also fit well with the overall business strategy and the improvement of the organization's development capability. Finally, they must ensure that the rest of the organization upholds its commitments to the team, and to the future rewards and careers of those serving on the team. Only senior managers can collectively be the commitment manager, for the senior management perspective is uniquely that of the project portfolio and the business as a whole.

Sponsor/Coach

In this role, senior management helps project teams deal with unforeseen contingencies. Some of these may motivate a reassessment of the project's boundaries; others will pertain to internal team operations. All such contingencies create potential areas of conflict and novel situations ripe for innovation or error. In the role of sponsor/coach, senior management advises the team, providing wisdom from years of experience.

When difficulties arise within the team's operations—whether it be a personality conflict, disagreements within the group over team direction, or a personal performance issue—the sponsor may become a sounding board for the team leader, listening, providing ideas, and helping the leader to clarify issues and sharpen the options for action. When contingencies arise that affect the boundaries of the project—e.g., a need for new features, resource constraints, changes in systems—the sponsor can be quite useful in helping the team see the issues in light of the overall business and the needs of senior management.

A key role for the sponsor/coach, therefore, is to help the core team identify the areas in which it has decision-making authority and those in which it is subject to senior management review—and to communicate contingencies to senior management in ways that are understandable. So, for example, early on in the project, the sponsor might meet with the team to clarify where senior management's concerns lie and how the team should alert the sponsor to changes from plan. Key areas might include:

Leading Product Development

- Resource commitments beyond those in the contract book.
- Pricing decisions for major customers.
- Potential deviations from major scheduling dates.
- New requirements in the marketplace.

In this role, the sponsor/coach represents senior management in its ongoing, day-to-day dealings with the team. Senior management speaks to the team as Senior Management, through the sponsor. This is crucial. Senior management needs to speak in one voice when it speaks as Senior Management. Members of senior management will, of course, speak as heads of functions to the team through the functional leaders and other members of the team. But Senior Management has only one voice, and that is the voice of the sponsor. Establishing this role, therefore, reinforces senior management's need to work as a team and to provide leadership that is complete and consistent in its direction. Doing charters and contract books is a powerful way of setting the framework for the team. But in the inevitably changing circumstances of a dynamic world, both the team and senior management need a way to resolve uncertainty and, for real-time issues, to clarify a course of action that is effective for the team and for the enterprise. That is the role of the senior management sponsor.

Process Improver

As the owner and creator of the development process, senior management is also responsible for improving its performance. Senior management is in a unique position to play this role. It is, of course, important for everyone in the organization to look for opportunities to learn from their own involvement as well as about the way the process operates in general. But learning about development and using insights derived from that learning to improve the firm's development processes will not occur naturally as individuals in the organization learn. That is, organizational learning does not happen simply because individuals learn. Two aspects of product development make learning especially difficult and position senior management to play the role of process improver.

- Development projects are complex, with activity going on in many different locations, involving many different people, over extended periods of time. The outcomes that matter are often ambiguous. They are the result of complex interactions that cut across specific functional groups or specific individuals.
- Once a project is complete, all the pressure in the organization is to move on to the next activity. Taking time to reflect on experience and learn is unlikely to occur under the normal press of events.

Because of these factors, learning about product development and improving the performance of the development process are unlikely to occur without leadership. They will require concerted, systematic effort directed and focused by senior managers who have the requisite vantage point (the ability to see the whole) and perspective (the longer-term health of the enterprise).

To play the role of process improver, senior management must establish learning as a highly valued activity within the organization. But it must also take specific action to identify opportunities for improvement, to focus attention and effort on developing and implementing solutions, and to ensure that what is learned and proposed is in fact captured by the organization. The challenge for senior management is to cut through the complexity of product development to find the problems whose solution will lead to long-term improvement and performance. Senior managers who succeed in that effort use a team approach to uncover critical problems and search for root causes. The insight that emerges from that search, in turn, becomes the basis for changes in the way development gets done. Indeed, the way the organization "remembers" what it learns from its development experience is by capturing that learning through changes in procedures, tools, process, structure, and principles. To improve the process, senior management must lead a process not only of learning, but also of remembering and applying.

Learning about the behavior of the development process requires a conscious effort on the part of senior management as well as many others within the organization. But that effort to learn (and to remember) itself requires structure and organization if it is to have energy and coherence. We have found the project audit—a systematic project review conducted by a cross-functional team—particularly useful in organizing the search for understanding and in garnering the insight from specific projects. The project audit, headed by the project leader, involves individuals from all the key functions representing development. Under the direction of senior management, the cross-functional team reviews the project, conducts interviews with participants at all levels, and gathers data about project execution and performance. The team searches for patterns, identifies root causes, and develops recommendations for change that will capture what they have learned.

Learning from development projects—and thus playing the role of process improver—is one of the most difficult roles senior management takes on. It requires a willingness to make hard choices. Because what senior management needs to learn (and remember) cuts across individuals, work groups, and functions to encompass the development system as a whole, and because the phenomena it focuses on are complex and ambiguous, learning needs leadership. Indeed, it needs to be organized, managed, focused, and directed by leaders with skill, tenacity, and perspective.

Summary

The four roles of senior management in project execution are closely related to the progress of a project—launch, energy, commitments, contingencies. Each role addresses a connection between the project and the business as a whole. Like the front-end roles laid out in Chapter 3, senior management's roles in project execution are fundamentally focused on the relationship between the parts and the whole. The challenge of leadership here is balance: between team scope and senior management direction; between functional excellence and team performance; between what's right for the team and what's right for the business.

As always, senior management must keep an eye on the whole and the future while shaping and influencing the parts in the present. Building on the foundation of a solid front-end process, and in a context defined by Stage 4 functions, the roles laid out here provide an effective framework in which to exercise that kind of leadership. They also provide, collectively, a way for the organization to learn (and to consistently capture and apply that learning), so that each new project benefits to the maximum extent possible from those that have gone before.

In the end, the rate of organizational learning will determine whether or not a firm will increasingly experience new product development as a distinctive, sustainable advantage. And the effectiveness with which senior management carries out the leadership roles we have identified will drive that organizational learning. Thus, the rate and thoroughness with which senior management learns those roles, becomes confident and comfortable in applying them, and helps other team members do likewise is the essence of the challenge.

In the next chapter, we look at how a business within Kodak met a serious, even threatening, competitive challenge by establishing the kind of development approach we advocate. Senior management leadership was critical at every step of the way.

5

Leadership in Action: Developing Single-Use Cameras at Kodak

When product development is led by senior management, the whole is far more than the sum of its parts. With product development at the center of the business, a solid foundation in strategy and product planning, focused projects tied to the strategy and the architecture, and teams that work effectively, development performance can be dramatically and consistently excellent. The effect is a stream of well-timed and well-positioned products that are executed effectively, create momentum in the market, and build the enterprise.

In previous chapters we have examined the elements of a comprehensive approach to senior management leadership of product development. Here we look at a comprehensive illustration of how a single business integrated the elements into a distinctive development approach that created a series of very successful products and built an outstanding business. Our purpose here is to see the ideas of the prior chapters in action and to gain perspective on the impact of product development not just on a single project, but on a whole series of projects over time.

The product in the story is Eastman Kodak Company's FunSaver™, a single-use camera. Senior management leadership was crucial to the FunSaver's success. Senior managers set the direction, rhythm, pattern, and organizational expectations; they owned the development procedures, creating and investing in new tools and directly influencing how work got done. Kodak senior managers were directly involved in architecting the product line and building a portfolio of projects. They established the environment that attracted, nurtured, and strengthened specific types of people and focused their efforts to create new organizational capabilities. They managed the launch of the FunSaver projects and the portfolio of commitments, and sponsored and coached individual projects. As we tell the story, we will pause from time to time to comment on the actions taken and decisions made, as well as on the principles of leading product development adopted and followed by senior management.

The FunSaver Projects

In 1988, Kodak introduced the FunSaver, a basic single-use camera. The FunSaver was designed as a platform-type product; from the very beginning, the team that took charge of the business recognized that although a single-use camera represented a new kind of product for Kodak, one that would be designed, produced, and retailed differently, introducing it would not represent a break with the company's past—Kodak had long been in the camera business. However, the fact that it was a platform-type project also indicated that a new manufacturing process would be needed. Furthermore, the competitive environment into which it would be placed required development capabilities very different from those demanded in Kodak's very successful film business.

Once the FunSaver was introduced, derivative products (the Panoramic™, which sported a panoramic lens and provided a double-wide finished print, and the Weekend™, which was encased in a clear waterproof plastic outer shell) were rolled out. Within two years of the original camera's introduction, Kodak began working on a flash version of the FunSaver, a next-generation platform whose design incorporated recyclability, as well as additional derivatives based on that platform.

How these single-use cameras came into existence—the product development process established by Kodak for this emerging business—is an excellent example of how a clear strategy and well-designed product line architecture can lead to rapidly executed projects whose results are consistently successful in the market. Moreover, the business was able to do this while making the kinds of dramatic organizational changes needed for heavyweight team-based product development to operate effectively in an organizational setting that historically had emphasized functionally based team structures.

At Kodak, in a rolling series of efforts, both the original platform camera (the FunSaver) and two derivative products went from concept to development project to the marketplace *in 18 months;* the actual development project itself took fewer than 12 months. The second generation and its derivatives, leveraging learning from the original effort, significantly reduced that time even further.

The Challenge

When Kodak began its conquest of the single-use camera market in early 1987, the company was organized as a traditional, functional structure employing thousands of professionals in engineering, research and development, design, manufacturing, marketing, and so forth. A typical major development project took three years or more to complete; the process was highly functional, with each function performing the various development tasks sequentially. The company was attempting to quicken the pace of this functional approach by streamlining decision making. Its newly introduced manufacturing acceptance process (MAP) was to clarify which function had responsibility at which point in a project's development time, what was required at various milestones, and how responsibilities would shift once the milestones were reached. While the MAP approach was certainly an improvement over its predecessor, the FunSaver business team took a different approach with its set of projects, and delivered a quantum leap in performance and process.

Given the talent throughout the Kodak organization, many ideas were always being bandied about. Moreover, engineers could dedicate 10% of their time to "noodling"—pursuing new ideas they thought had particular promise and merit. Over the years, noodling had produced several important ideas related to single-use cameras. (Single-use cameras came loaded with film; when the film was exposed, both camera and film were taken to a photofinisher, who developed the film and, before Kodak's recyclable line, threw the camera away.)

Cameras and camera equipment had historically been part of the film group at Kodak. Because the gross margins on film were very high (estimated to be in the 80% range by some financial analysts), it was feared that a single-use camera would cannibalize film sales—replacing excellent margins with more average margins. To the extent that such substitutions occurred, this would have serious profit consequences indeed. The concern transcended margins, however. Kodak prided itself on its excellent film quality, and it knew exactly how to achieve and measure that quality consistently. Putting Kodak film into an inexpensive, plastic, single-use camera could result in second-rate photographs, something the company had experienced in an early version of a single-use camera that used 110 film (one of Kodak's traditional strongholds). That camera, introduced in the mid-1980s, produced blurred pictures, exhibited other quality problems, and received limited Kodak backing, resulting in limited market success (and eventual discontinuation).

Given this background, single-use camera ideas were routinely rejected and remained only at a technical exploration level; they represented, at best, advanced development (not commercial) ideas. One Kodak designer, however, had zealously worked on a 35mm single-use camera in his spare time for years, and had even estimated the variable costs to design and produce it.

Meanwhile, the market was moving to simpler, more automatic cameras using 35mm film; in the past, these had been expensive and difficult to operate, though they produced much higher-quality results than the 110 units. By the mid-1980s, Japanese 35mm cameras, which were relatively inexpensive, easy to use, and directed at the mass consumer market, entered the scene. This benefited sales of Kodak's 35mm film and processing equipment. Unfortunately, it benefited Japan's Fuji PhotoFilm as well. By the mid-1980s, Fuji had test marketed in Japan a single-use 35mm camera; in February 1987, it previewed this Quicksnap™ camera at a U.S. conference of photographic equipment dealers, indicating that it would be available in volume in Japan within the following six months and in the U.S. sometime after that. Fuji's announcement brought Kodak's competitive, market, and technical challenge into sharp focus.

Kodak's Response

Because Kodak did substantial business in Japan, it was well aware of Fuji's single-use camera and the threat it posed. Fuji's product was positioned in Japan as an entry-level camera for young people and others who could not afford the more expensive 35mm offerings, which retailed (in Japan) for $150 and up. While single-use cameras represented a niche market, the fact that people actually bought and used them proved that a market existed. Kodak would have to respond.

Kodak's senior management made two critical decisions at this juncture. First, it moved the camera group out from under the film group and into its consumer products area. This not only gave the camera people more autonomy, it provided them with better access to senior management because they now reported to a higher level in the organization. Second, senior managers recognized that if Kodak was to create a successful, high-margin (low cost) single-use 35mm camera to compete with Fuji, it needed to change the way it handled new product development. Strong team-based product development would be a must.

At the same time, senior management established a small group of marketing people who were to determine (a) if Kodak should enter the single-use market; (b) how it could do it; and (c) how it could do it given the two major problems of film gross margins (potential profit cannibalization) and picture quality. Very quickly the marketing team asked Kodak's lens group to determine if it was possible to come up with an inexpensive plastic lens that also produced good-quality pictures. Shortly thereafter, the lens group discovered a plastic lens that not only produced good quality inexpensively, it could create a wide-angle picture of even better quality than the regular-size picture. (This became known as the "double-wide" or "panoramic" format.)

Comments

Kodak's response to the opportunity in single-use cameras illustrates the process of evaluating ideas and shaping them into projects. Because engineers could spend 10% of their time on noodling, they had already explored several good ideas related to single-use camera technology. However, because the camera group had reported to the film group, the latter's concerns about margins and quality predominated when it came to single-use ideas. Besides, they had been burned (with the 110 single-use product) once before in the marketplace. This set up a vicious cycle: ideas could never advance beyond technical exploration because of the film group's concerns, and because the ideas never advanced, they never reached the point at which they could disprove those concerns.

- In essence, ideas got trapped in the wide end of the development funnel, never to make it to a potential project stage. Moreover, because there were no projects whose basic positioning had been outlined via product line architecture, there was literally no place for these ideas to go.

Once the Fuji threat materialized, senior management recognized that those margin and quality issues had to be reopened and reconsidered. That is, because the competitive threat was deemed so significant, the old order had to change if the threat was to be met head-on. The key driver was timing. If Kodak was to challenge Fuji on the single-use front, it would have to fight for shelf space immediately. In small retail outlets in the U.S., for example, only one brand of single-use cameras was likely to be displayed, and if Fuji got first-mover advantage—even if Kodak came up with a better version subsequently—it could be too late. Thus, the development of a competitive product would be driven by a precise target date for market introduction, which implied that Kodak's traditional product development process would have to change.

- Senior management recognized that it would have to take charge of development: it would have to own the process and manage it. It would have to set the agenda and ensure that it was followed.

Moving the camera group out from under the film division enabled senior management to determine if there was, in fact, a business for Kodak to nurture in the single-use market (i.e., without jeopardizing margins or quality). The move, then, enabled senior management to look at the single-use camera as a potential product, not just a "delivery system" (and a presumed inadequate one at that) for Kodak 35mm film. Setting up the focused marketing group furthered the evaluation process; that group quickly had R&D form what we would call an advanced development project to come up with a lens solution. Not only did that project find a solution, it discovered the attractiveness of a double-wide format, which ultimately turned into the first derivative product off the basic single-use camera platform. Senior management was now in a position to give the go-ahead for the project—and to take the important step of making it a team-based effort.

- In other words, senior management was poised to launch the project and the team.

These actions do, in fact, capture the essence of the development funnel process. Ideas were explored both in light of the business (how to deal with the Fuji threat and margins/quality concerns) and in the context of opportunities and constraints (ideas related to single-use technology and how development had heretofore "worked" within the business). Senior management evaluated ideas and determined the extent of their readiness for incorporation into a commercial project. A subgroup (the marketing group) was quickly formed to explore the feasibility of the various ideas that had been generated in the past, and it commissioned what was essentially an advanced development project in the lens group. All this information clarified the nature of a possible FunSaver platform and set the stage for the launch of a cross-functional team to commercialize it.

The Cross-Functional Team

Once the feasibility of making an inexpensive, high-quality single-use camera had been determined, the consumer product group's senior management set up a cross-functional team to lead the development effort. These six or so core people were dedicated to the project, and they, along with their senior management counterparts, drew up and agreed to operate under the following mandate:

- The camera's quality had to equal that of Kodak's standard 35mm offering.
- It had to be extremely reliable and not appear "cheap."
- It had to retail at a very low price (about $8, or under $5 wholesale).
- It had to preserve substantial margins (approaching $2, Kodak's margin on a roll of film).
- It had to be ready for market within 40 weeks.

Because the lens group had discovered the double-wide ("panoramic") format possibility already, senior managers and the team immediately understood that they were looking at the development of a product family—initially a platform *and* a derivative product. This added one more element to the above mandate: the entire product family had to be manufacturable on a single, cost-effective product line. The interrelated questions to be faced immediately were those of sequencing and timing. In terms of sequencing, the panoramic model (derivative) could be made and introduced first, with the basic version (platform) following, or vice versa. The issue of timing included not only when the two products would be introduced in relation to one another, but when they should be introduced in relation to each other in the U.S., Europe, and elsewhere (particularly in Fuji's home territory, Japan).

It was decided to introduce the basic camera—the FunSaver I—first in the U.S., and then follow it shortly thereafter with the panoramic model. (That model was anticipated to be popular in Japan; it was distinctive and could be patented.) Therefore, once the development team had done most of its work on the platform, it would quickly turn to the derivative and complete its design in short order.

Concurrent with these decisions about product line architecture, the development team began to focus on issues of manufacturing. At the outset of the project, the team understood that a new manufacturing process (a "platform") would be needed and that the camera's design had to be simple and inexpensive to produce with consistently high quality. Design and manufacturing tasks had to be carefully integrated. The mold tooling for a part could not be designed until the part itself was designed, yet tooling characteristics affected part design. At the same time, the degree of automation of the manufacturing process had to be selected, and like tooling design, that choice depended on the volume of parts to be manufactured. But to estimate volumes, always highly uncertain on a new product, marketing needed a good estimate of the manufacturing cost.

To deal with these challenges, a manufacturing engineer was co-located with several parts designers and a tool designer, all of whom were dedicated to the project. Using a new, sophisticated CAD/CAM system—a tool whose adoption was supported and championed by a key member of the senior management team— the project team was able to develop the tooling and the parts simultaneously. With the CAD system, designers could see the fit of their respective parts, product designers and tool makers could see how their tasks interacted, and part manufacturing people could easily gain early access to part and tool design decisions, enabling them to estimate costs and identify and evaluate automation options.

The team decided early on to do a lot of prototyping (which the CAD system facilitated). This helped get the attention of people throughout the organization: here was a tangible product (and a high-quality one at that), not a piece of paper. But this early proto-typing served another purpose. It revealed the camera's resemblance to the Instamatic, of which Kodak had sold millions, and therefore formed a basis for comparison that enabled thorough financial modeling. The single-use camera, in effect, was an Instamatic that was used only once. And, serendipitously, the early prototyping activity led to a second derivative product, in addition to the planned panoramic model.

Part of the prototype testing included loaning the models to Kodak employees for use over the weekend, then processing their film and getting their feedback. One designer on the team, who borrowed a prototype, got the camera wet while he was on a kayaking trip. He knew that if the film remained wet, the pictures he'd already taken could be developed; if the film dried out it would be ruined. So he returned the camera on Monday morning in a plastic bag full of water, and sure enough, the pictures he had taken came out all right. But this triggered a thought within the

Leading Product Development

Figure 5-1
FunSaver I Project Plans

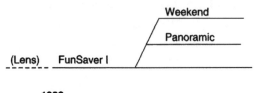

Product and Process Development Projects

team: maybe the camera should be in a "plastic bag." Thus, the waterproof single-use camera (subsequently named the Weekend) was born. The idea was to have the basic camera covered in a clear plastic sheath as it came off the end of the production line. The process involved adding a step at the final production station; there was no basic redesign needed of either the product or the process. Figure 5–1 shows at an aggregate level the product map and the manufacturing process.

When the team contemplated this second derivative, it already was part way through the platform project. But it decided that because production for this derivative would be the same except for the final step, the schedules for the other two products should be adjusted. The waterproof version provided a substantial opportunity. 35mm cameras, traditionally expensive and somewhat tricky to use, were carefully protected by most camera owners, particularly in risky environments like the beach and on boats. With a waterproof camera, the risk would be eliminated: taking pictures in these environments could be safe, fun, and inexpensive. Figure 5–2 indicates the mix of product and process—the portfolio of projects—according to the degree of change involved.

Figure 5–2

Mix of Product and Process Development Projects (FunSaver I)

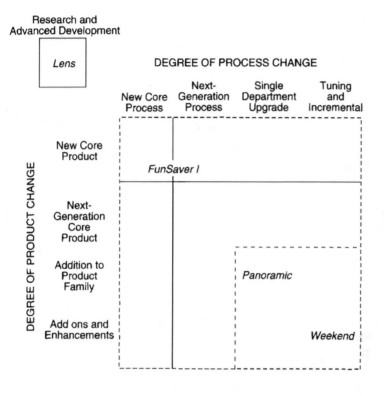

At this point in the project's development, the team made a crucial decision: the derivatives, though not expected to be major volume items, in fact would be the "carriers" of advertising, promotion, and the like. The panoramic model was not only unique, it took better pictures. The waterproof version was also unique and would expand opportunities for taking pictures. So the team decided that the derivatives should be disproportionately promoted, because they would be the attention getters and would further distinguish Kodak's line from Fuji's offerings.

Comments

What Kodak's senior management and the project team accomplished in their first few months was not only significant but dramatic, given the vast change it represented from Kodak's traditional development approach. Recall that Kodak's manufacturing acceptance process had only recently been introduced, and, moreover, that it was dedicated to streamlining a functional development process. With the FunSaver project, not only did the organization move to a team-based process, it moved to what we would call a *heavyweight* team approach. This approach accounted for much of the speed and integration of this development effort, while accommodating and encouraging substantial marketing, design, and manufacturing innovation.

These achievements highlight the value of having a group of empowered, cross-functional people dedicated to a project. It also reveals what happens when such a team is supported, encouraged, and guided by senior managers assuming new roles.

Senior managers set the direction, as noted earlier, both by deciding to develop single-use cameras in the first place, and then by moving the project into the camera group. They took responsibility for the development process, changing how things would be done (by a cross-functional, co-located team), identifying the tools that would support such efforts (such as a new CAD/CAM system), and becoming intensely involved in all aspects of development. For example, collectively, they were the chief architect of the product line, establishing what would be introduced and when. And they were the project/team launcher.

With this senior management guidance, the team assumed considerable responsibility for shaping the development of the project, fully aware of its demanding business and production goals. The team knew what it had to do and the time frame in which it had to be accomplished. And while the mandate the team accepted and worked from was a combination of charter and contract book (something that became more sharply differentiated in the FunSaver II effort), the goals were clear, achievable, and motivating.

The team very quickly recognized that decisions on designing, producing, and selling a product family needed to be considered simultaneously (and they all had to be made in the context of Kodak's business goals and the target date for the base camera's introduction). Thus, even in a technically driven operation (which characterized much of this development), marketing had full say and was highly influential. The team and senior management were also sufficiently flexible that when the waterproof camera idea cropped up, they could recognize its value, define and evaluate it, recalibrate the overall project schedule and resources, and rethink the marketing of the entire family of products to be offered. Such timing and sequencing of a platform and its derivatives are the essence of product line architecting.

The project team—dedicated, co-located, and using superior support tools—was able to move swiftly in developing parts, tooling, and the manufacturing process, keeping engineering change orders to a minimum. Because this team was empowered, it redefined tasks and their timing, sequence, and ownership with relative ease and without significant delays. Moreover, because the product line architecture had been established, the team could do these tasks for the platform and the derivatives concurrently. This ensured not only that the derivative projects could be done more quickly, it meant that they captured significant cost savings and leveraged fully the work done on the platform product and process.

Critical to the above was senior management's role as energy source. The team was given resources to draw upon—people and support—for all three products (the FunSaver and the two derivatives) so that the development of all three could move together, as warranted. This was possible because senior management was involved from the beginning (setting direction, owning the development process, launching the project/team, and focusing on providing what the team needed to succeed).

It was also clear that senior management was playing the roles of sponsor/coach and commitment manager. The early prototyping was an inspired approach. It gained buy-in and commitment across the organization, particularly at the top; it created the financial modeling that enabled people to understand how this project was aligned with and built on previous efforts (particularly the Instamatic); it helped build consensus within the team and outside—everyone had something tangible to deal with. And by providing prototypes for employees to test and following up on how they reacted to them, the product was further refined and potential problems were addressed early on. (Even if the waterproof idea had not arisen, this prototyping step would still have been critical to the project's successful unfolding.)

In their sponsor/coach role and in their commitment manager role, senior managers helped the team incorporate the

Weekend idea swiftly into the overall project plan, providing additional resources and reconfiguring the product line architecture. One can only imagine what would happen to serendipitous ideas like the waterproof camera in a functionally oriented development process. Even if it were possible to identify such an option and to get swift senior management approval, a scramble for resources would surely ensue, and the net result would probably be a situation of robbing Peter to pay Paul. Instead, because of senior management involvement, the team was able to seize the opportunity and run with it.

Thus, in a short period of time, a handful of people representing various functions within the camera group at Kodak made major decisions in a wide range of areas and oversaw their enactment, all under the sponsorship, coaching, and guidance of senior management. This is the hallmark of heavyweight team-based product development and the role senior managers play in making it work. The time line for the formal development portion of the FunSaver project appears in Figure 5–3.

The Next-Generation FunSaver

The original product line architecture plan called for introducing the FunSaver in 1988, with the Panoramic and Weekend versions to follow a few months thereafter; a second generation, built around a single-use camera with a flash, would come out in 1991. (Fuji had introduced its QuickSnap Flash™ in the U.S. shortly after the FunSaver debuted.) However, the FunSaver turned out to be extremely successful, capturing about 70% of the U.S. sin-

Leading Product Development

Figure 5–3
FunSaver I Project Time Line

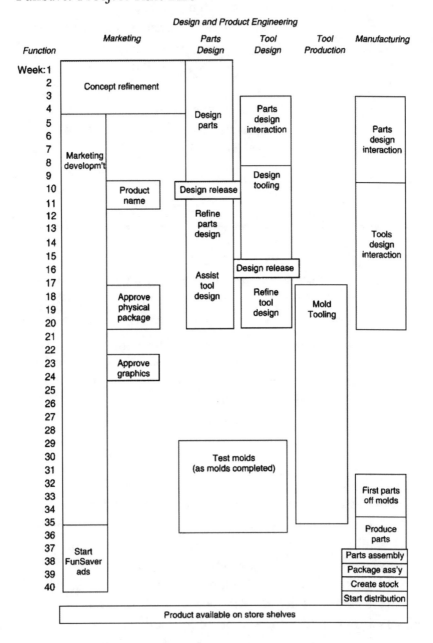

gle-use market by late 1989, and the derivatives were quite popular in both the U.S. and Japan. As a consequence, the payback for the project was much faster than anticipated, thereby removing part of the financial rationale for holding off the second generation family of designs until 1991.

Though highly popular in the U.S. and Japan, single-use cameras did not take off in Europe, primarily because of recycling concerns. These had been voiced in the U.S. as well, but not as strongly. In fact, the original name of the FunSaver had been Fling, but very quickly the name took on negative connotations (of a wasteful, throwaway product) and was immediately changed. Further, even though Kodak offered to pay photofinishers return shipping costs to encourage them to send back the used cameras, which the company would melt down to reclaim the plastic, photofinishers tended to throw them away.

Thus, a combination of factors prompted senior management to assemble a cross-functional core team in 1989 to plan the development and introduction of the next-generation family of cameras in 1990. It was decided that the family would include a FunSaver with a flash as the platform, and three derivatives: the base model without the flash, the Panoramic, and the Weekend. The entire family would be produced on a single production line and would be recyclable. This meant that the FunSaver II project would have three major integrated parts: the product, the manufacturing process, and the recycling system.

The team decided to use the same manufacturing facility used for the current FunSaver models, with an upgraded production line that would accommodate the new platform and its derivatives. The challenge was significant. In effect, the team had to design the three subsystems of the platform concurrently: one for the product, another for the manufacturing process, and a third for the recycling process. It then had to convert the original FunSaver production line to the new one, while continuing to manufacture

Leading Product Development

the "old" Panoramic and Weekend models. This was all accomplished, and the FunSaver Flash was introduced in late 1990, with the recyclable nonflash, Panoramic, and Weekend versions coming shortly thereafter. By 1992, the family was selling in excess of 25 million units worldwide on an annual basis. It offered a full product line, had significant market positions worldwide, and its unit margins were comparable to the margins on film. Finally, much to Kodak's delight, there was no impact on existing film sales.

Moreover, the product family spawned another derivative offspring: a portrait camera used for close-ups that included a "fill-in" flash. On this version, the flash was positioned at the end of the camera with a small flip top that reflected light indirectly, rather than directly, onto the subject. The purpose of this indirect flash was to fill in shadows around the subject's face.

All told, by mid-1994, Kodak's single-use camera products were being sold at a rate of more than 60 million units a year; the company had introduced a number of derivatives aimed at specific subsegments, market niches, or specialized distribution channels; and Kodak was expanding its variety of packaging and promotions for parties and special events.

Comments

Behind the decision to go with a next-generation FunSaver, and to do so one year ahead of plan, lies a series of extremely important issues that senior management and the project team had to wrestle with in a timely manner. That these issues could be successfully resolved in such a short period highlights the importance of having a product development and manufacturing process architecture and the capability to move from ideas to projects quickly. It also shows how the learning from one project can be leveraged by transferring it to the next. Underlying these strengths was the ability to frame and address key issues in a timely and effective manner.

One central issue the team confronted was whether the Flash model should be simply an enhanced derivative of the original FunSaver I. Basically, if the Flash model was created off the initial platform, it would have a higher unit cost and therefore a lower margin per unit; additionally, it would not be recyclable. But making the Flash a next-generation platform meant investing significantly in effort and resources sooner than originally planned, plus writing off part of the remaining investment in the current line.

The arguments for the Flash as derivative were powerful. Not only was Fuji's flash camera already on the market, but introducing a competitive product as a derivative would take Kodak as little as 26 weeks. The FunSaver platform was not yet two years old, and the current assembly line had yet to reach capacity. If the Flash were a derivative, capacity would be reached—and the costs of the project's development could be covered easily. Finally, although many improvements in the FunSaver line had been made already, more would surely come. A derivative Flash, therefore, would allow the team more time to devise additional improvements in the first year of Flash production, all of which could be used to benefit the next-generation platform, scheduled for 1991.

Yet the design of the flash was not trivial. Its electronics, which included a circuit board, could not easily be incorporated into the current FunSaver I, and therefore represented a significant investment and a potential risk in quality. Pricing would be a problem too, since Fuji's flash camera retailed only slightly above its nonflash version and the basic Fun-

Saver I. It was estimated, therefore, that Kodak's margins on the Flash-as-derivative would be only three-quarters of the FunSaver's.

On the other hand, with the Flash as a platform, the margins would be an estimated 25% higher, due primarily to eliminating the design and manufacturing problems that had been identified since the FunSaver I project. Of course, designing a new platform and process would cost a lot and take about two to four months longer than the derivative option. Moreover, the team anticipated that the FunSaver II, as a non-Flash derivative of the Flash platform, would actually be the highest-volume product, and that raised concerns. Would designing a new platform based on the Flash adversely affect the cost or quality of the higher-volume, more basic non-Flash product?

Yet the new design could incorporate recycling, and that represented a major competitive advantage—in the U.S., Japan, and particularly Europe, which had yet to be penetrated by a single-use camera. A redesigned FunSaver would provide a better "system solution" as well, since the entire camera would support the flash. Finally, the platform would allow a new set of recyclable derivatives to be developed.

A major concern with the platform choice, however, involved current derivatives. The new platform's production line would have to be designed so that the existing Panoramic and Weekend models could be produced on it. Yet that might constrain the design of the new platform and not take maximum advantage of the improvements that had been already identified. It would be possible to produce old and new versions on separate lines, but that would complicate manufacturing and would cost more than having only one line. Finally, the team needed to determine how much of the new platform's production line could be postponed until the Panoramic and Weekend were redesigned based on the FunSaver Flash, and what portion of capital costs that would represent.

The last factor that needed to be weighed was the timing and sequencing of the redesigned derivatives (which would impact decisions about production line design). This timing/sequence decision entailed looking at both the effect of the derivatives on the market and the development issues themselves, including manufacturing concerns. The choice boiled down to two options. First, the derivatives could precede the release of the new platform products as a "second wave." The derivatives would have certain features to be subsequently incorporated into the new platform. The second option was to have the new derivatives immediately follow the second-generation platform product, the approach taken in the original FunSaver project. Senior management and the team decided to choose the second option; Figure 5–4 shows how the product and process generation projects for the FunSaver II effort

Figure 5–4
FunSaver II Project Plans

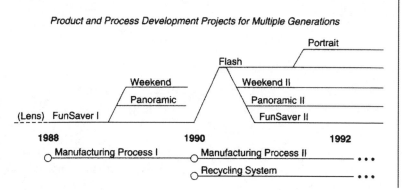

Product and Process Development Projects for Multiple Generations

unfolded. Figure 5–5 shows how the effort looked from the perspective of the portfolio and mix of product/process change projects.

Figure 5–5
Mix of Product and Process Development Projects (FunSaver II)

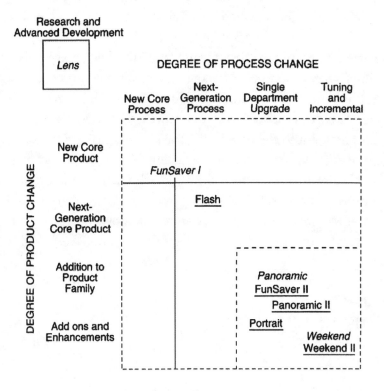

All these highly complex issues were, as suggested, tightly interwoven. Product line architecture choices affected product design choices, which influenced tooling choices, which affected process design choices, which were influenced by the architecture choices (e.g., time to market affected manufacturing volume), and so on. Threading through these decisions were resource allocation and capacity constraint or underutilization concerns, investment choices, and make/buy decisions. Being able to "connect the dots" demanded both a functioning development strategy and senior management leadership. It was not enough to have a good product design team, a good manufacturing team, and a good marketing team—they had to work together, in an integrated and seamless fashion, to accomplish what Kodak did. And they had to be empowered to do so.

Putting the Pieces Together

Reviewing Kodak's accomplishments on the FunSaver projects shows how senior management can rapidly build a business based on integrated, superior product development. Perspective was crucial. Consider, for example, the issue of margins and quality, which broadened in a few short years. Any mention of single-use cameras prior to the FunSaver project drew a negative response bacause of their presumed threat to the film business' very high margins and to Kodak's reputation for very high quality. By the time of the FunSaver Flash project, both margins and quality were naturally ongoing concerns in the derivative versus platform debate, but they were part of a broader discussion. Moreover, senior management's ability to see the whole shifted the focus from margins within a single product to returns over the life of a family of products. Senior management also shifted quality concerns from the performance of the film to the performance of the camera and its design and consistent manufacturability. Finally, by opening up the discussion of margins and quality, Kodak basically opened up the movement of ideas from noodling to commercial potential.

The decision to move the camera group out from under the film group was critical to this change, but many other things reinforced it—for instance, the decision to make system prototypes early on. The prototypes themselves were enabled by the decision to use the CAD/CAM system (it was possible to move more swiftly to a point where prototypes could be built); this was made more effective by co-locating the design team, whose members, in turn, included people from manufacturing and tooling. Thus, the early prototypes did not simply represent a design idea that might be manufacturable; they were something much more complete, and many of their manufacturing aspects already had been verified.

Early prototyping "proved" that an inexpensive, high-quality, single-use camera that could be manufactured quickly and in high volumes was feasible. It had the added benefit of revealing the camera's relation to Kodak's very successful Instamatic offering, thereby provoking important financial modeling based on that product.

Fuji's QuickSnap made clear the competitive challenge for the FunSaver team, but the reality of a 35mm single-use camera prototype crystallized what an effective Kodak initiative would look like. Thus, in shaping the product line architecture, senior management and the FunSaver team were not simply laying out their future hopes for product development or positioning the business in relation to Fuji (i.e., producing "me too" versions). The business strategy, in essence, was a clear-cut decision to conquer the single-use market. The architecture that emerged was designed to position a line of cameras in a way that would effectively counter the Fuji offering, and then leapfrog Fuji with unique derivatives.

Significantly, while the near-term impetus for the FunSaver was meeting the Fuji threat directly, the goal itself stretched when architecting came into play: it became making the original camera a platform from which the team could develop unique derivative versions. At the same time, having the panoramic possibility identified early in the concept evaluation stage encouraged thinking in terms of a product family. The product line architecture would not have been possible (and certainly not within the 40-week time frame) without the advantage of information, ideas, and capability available within the organization: the double-wide lens, the water-proof housing, and CAD technology for rapid prototyping. This was a two-way street. Senior management set the direction and defined the broad business objectives, but the early findings in lens technology and product cost helped shape the architecture. Likewise, senior management had to ensure that the FunSaver team had access to critical ideas and information, as well as the resources and capability to carry out the work. In turn, early results of the team's work helped shape the timing and content of the product line.

Timing was everything in the FunSaver project. The ability to shape the architecture rapidly, incorporate new ideas, and hit the market window was directly influenced by senior management's decision to break with the past and change its development process—from the traditional functional, sequential approach to a team-based approach. Obviously, this was not a spur of the moment choice, and many issues beyond the FunSaver project were involved. But the fact remains that without the crucial decision and commitment to do the FunSaver in a brand-new way, the project team would not have bought into the project's ambitious goals and the product would not have hit its market introduction date or met its other aggressive performance targets.

Kodak's team-based product development was heavyweight team-based development. In the FunSaver project, core team members not only came from different functions, they also brought significant and varied experiences along with them (e.g., backgrounds that encompassed mechanical engineering, manufacturing, and consumer equipment product design). Thus, the team was intentionally composed of people with multiple skills and with broad authority within their respective areas. At the same time, these various skills and abilities could flourish because the team was allowed to make decisions and follow up on them. In the absence of this empowerment, being co-located, dedicated, and having the CAD support system would not have been nearly as effective. That is, giving a functional-type team or a lightweight team a CAD system simply means that each piece of the sequential process is done more efficiently. It does not guarantee either that the pieces will fit together along the way or that the results will be more successful than they would have been with the old system.

The CAD system was effective because of the team's cross-functional composition, particularly the incorporation of a manufacturing engineer and a tooling designer on the core team. At the same time, with marketing fully represented on the project team, product line architecture choices—which were fundamental to the myriad decisions involving product, tooling, and manufacturing process—could be made successfully the first time. Essentially, the entire FunSaver effort—both generations—was market-based. The point was not just to make a single-use camera, but to introduce a single-use camera by a specific date with a certain financial payoff, laying the foundation for subsequent products and an entire business.

The FunSaver team flourished in the context of strong functions striving to move their strategic role to Stage 4. A good example of this was the role of manufacturing in the FunSaver strategy. Concurrent with the project's formation, but unrelated to it, was a plan to subdivide Kodak's huge Elmgrove facility, a manufacturing plant in Rochester, New York, where Kodak is headquartered. The motivation for this plan was to focus manufacturing and enhance its contribution. The result was that manufacturing itself became subdivided; instead of one large organization and plant, manufacturing executives created product-focused plants within a plant, with a manufacturing manager for each. From these developments arose the idea of putting single-use camera production into Elmgrove (camera production was currently being outsourced) and having a manufacturing manager on the FunSaver core team. That manager, in turn, suggested putting a tooling designer on the team. All this happened very early in the project's time frame yet could not have occurred in the absence of strong functions and a heavyweight team structure—simultaneously connected to the functions and business organization, but empowered to work more or less independently within that structure. Being plugged in to things that were happening elsewhere at Kodak (e.g., at Elmgrove) enabled the FunSaver team to take advantage of them.

Having a strong manufacturing presence on the team was critical to the success of the project. A critical insight was that the process for manufacturing the cameras had to be designed along with the parts and tooling. This awareness was essential for rapid development to succeed. New platform projects inherently entail process changes, but too often these are handled separately, guaranteeing problems at the tail end of the project as manufacturing tries to gear up and handle myriad tasks in a manner consistent with and complementary to the product's design and overall business goals. When extensive planning and testing are done in the project's early stages and manufacturing is involved from the outset, most of these problems can be avoided or identified early and resolved quickly.

Not everything ran like clockwork in the FunSaver projects, of course. Changing the name from Fling to FunSaver three months after market introduction, for example, necessitated changes in packaging, advertising, and so forth. Additionally, the Panoramic and Weekend versions turned out to be less easily manufactured than anticipated, and not all photofinishers could process the Panoramic's double-wide format. And Kodak discovered that its cameras could be sold in many more places (such as convenience stores) than it had anticipated, entailing subsequent refinements in distribution and sales. But senior management learned from these and other problems, and when the FunSaver Flash project was initiated, it incorporated that learning.

Learning is perhaps the most striking aspect of this story. The FunSaver Flash project was vastly more sophisticated than the original project; it also was accomplished far more quickly. Senior management's ability to improve the process and manage a complete set of projects was crucial. The flash technology was complex, the process was complicated by the need to accommodate the original Panoramic and Weekend versions on the same line that would make the new Flash cameras, and the concurrent development of a worldwide recycling process was a venture into the unknown. None of these tasks could have been undertaken—much less undertaken simultaneously—without a process that integrated information and learning and coordinated the various projects through what we call the aggregate project plan.

If we look at senior management's actions in Kodak's FunSaver development effort, we see each of the critical tools and mechanisms, and the central roles that define effective senior management leadership: direction, architecture, portfolio, funnel, launch, energy, commitment, and sponsor/coach. Moreover, senior management integrated each element to achieve a coherent, comprehensive approach to development. Senior management discovered a rhythm: it saw how platforms and derivatives work from both a development and a market perspective. It gained a sense of platform life—the customer's willingness and ability to absorb "new" products, the competitive realities that pressed for dynamic change, and the organization's willingness and ability to move from the past to the future. And by changing the process and launching a heavyweight development team, it ensured that the product would draw on the best ideas in the business, that the business would have the capacity and capability to act on them, and that the ideas pursued would match and strengthen the business strategy. The result was a pattern of consistent excellence in developing FunSaver products.

This chapter has focused on one example of successful senior leadership in product development. The FunSaver story is a real-world illustration of how, over a very short period of time, a business can move from traditional, congested, sequential development to effective heavyweight teams that work on a solid foundation of product line architecture, aggregate project plans, and the development funnel. Getting there is not easy. But the view is more than worth the climb. The concluding chapter addresses the challenge of implementation for senior management—leading significant change in the structure and process of product development, and in the personal attitudes, behavior, and roles of senior managers.

6

Turning Promise into Reality

The first four chapters in this book introduced a range of tools and roles that enable a new approach to product development, and the preceding chapter showed how these elements fit together into a total system that can achieve remarkable results in a brief period of time. In this final chapter, we want to step back and provide a map for implementing an effective product development process in your organization.

The challenge for senior managers is to take action: to lead by making the right things happen, and to substantially change the performance of the development process. This is not easy. It raises all the usual problems of organizational change, including personal discomfort as individual roles and familiar procedures shift, along with issues of turf, politics, and personality. Effecting dramatic change in development performance is particularly difficult, however, because product development touches nearly everything the business does. Its very pervasiveness (even when done poorly) means that everyone within the enterprise is affected. Added to this is the fact that the problems confronting senior management in making the kinds of improvements we advocate are complex and inherently challenging. Solving such problems requires an ability to break them down, find the critical dimensions, craft solutions, and make them happen. Our intent in this chapter is to give senior managers the "traction" they need to make progress. Put another way, because the issues are so complex and difficult, without some kind of framework for implementation—a means of digging into the situation—senior managers will spin their wheels, progress will be exceedingly slow, and the temptation to throw in the towel will be correspondingly high.

With traction provided by a strong implementation framework, senior managers will be in a much better position to launch the changes needed to bring leadership to product development and substantially improve its performance. The changes are of two kinds. The first involves changing the processes and structure the organization uses to plan and execute the transformation of ideas into products, with special emphasis on senior management's role. This is the stuff of Chapters 3 and 4, and its impact is evident in the FunSaver story laid out in Chapter 5.

We begin the chapter by introducing two basic paths for implementing change in the process and structure of product development. The first path begins with project execution, on the right side of the attention/influence diagram (repeated in Figure 6–1). In particular, it focuses on implementing heavyweight teams. The second path originates from the left side of Figure 6–1, and focuses on the planning processes that underlie the product architecture, the funnel process, and the project portfolio. Each starting point creates a different dynamic in implementation, and thus each merits analysis.

The second kind of change required for leadership is personal, and involves the attitudes and behavior of individuals—most im-

Figure 6–1

Timing of Management Attention and Influence in Product
Development

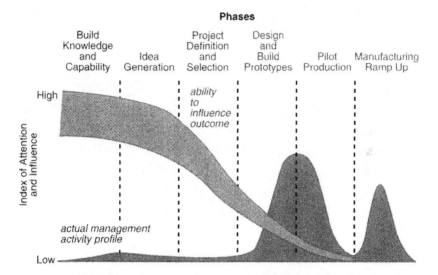

Source: S. C. Wheelwright and K. B. Clark, *Revolutionizing Product Development*
(New York: The Free Press, 1992) p. 33. See also F. Gluck and R. Foster,. "Managing Technological Change: A Box of Cigars for Brad." *Harvard Business Review*
(1976, September–October) p. 141.

portantly, senior managers. Changing what these key individuals
do makes the new process and structure work. Indeed, only when
there is tight integration between the new process and the attitudes and behavior of senior managers does product development
get the kind of leadership it needs.

Once we have outlined the two paths of implementation, we
discuss the attitudes and behavior of senior managers essential to
success no matter which path is chosen. In fact, getting senior
management understanding of and commitment to the changes
ahead is the crucial first step on either path. As the word "path"
suggests, implementation is a journey—and, as with any journey,

it is best to start out prepared. For senior management, preparation begins at home. Because so much of what matters in leading product development has to do with the attitudes and behavior of senior managers, it is essential that senior managers start with themselves.

But they also must make such changes as a group if the senior management team is to achieve consensus and a shared understanding of the way forward. Thus, the beginning of the journey, regardless of which direction it goes, must involve pulling all the senior managers together. No matter what specific actions the team decides to take or what changes it tries to introduce, unless the senior management group is integrated and of one mind about purposes, the changes likely to ensue, and the relative priorities to be accorded the task, the effort will flounder if not founder.

A key aspect of that shared understanding must be the stages of each function's strategic role and the power of moving to Stage 4. The journey of implementation in product development must be part of (and a motivating force behind) the move to create a Stage 4 enterprise. Because implementing the concepts and ideas we've introduced hinges so critically on senior management's role, it will become, by necessity, an educational process for senior managers. The shared understanding, therefore, is not only about desired processes and systems, but about the personal learning challenge each member of senior management will face. At the outset of the journey everyone must be ready to go to school. And everyone must be involved from the outset.

Defining the Improvement Path

Most firms have a number of projects already under way or about to start, providing a natural path for senior managers who seek to implement a new approach to product development. A focus on executing such projects more effectively provides an established setting in which to work, an opportunity for real impact in the not-too-distant future, and a vehicle for demonstrating senior management's commitment to the organization.

Existing projects, however, may lack the right definition or appropriate resources, and may already be heavily imbued with the firm's conventional practices. Such circumstances may suggest a path that starts instead with senior management's creating the right set of projects to be undertaken in, for example, the coming year. This directs attention to where influence can be great, to where less practice needs to be replaced, and to tasks the organization is more likely to view as strategic and thus appropriate for senior management involvement. Taking the planning path will affect performance on individual projects, but its impact may be less immediate and some of the existing projects may continue to be slow, over budget, and off target.

We will lay out the steps entailed for each path, and then return to the issue of how senior management should decide which to take. We will also examine the difference each path makes in the firm's long-term position.

Path 1: Implementing Heavyweight Teams

The major guideposts along this path are:

- Identifying a project whose charter, scope, and potential impact make it a good candidate for a heavyweight team.
- Forming a heavyweight team and selecting a project leader who can identify with the project and its goals and has the stature, skills, and abilities to lead the team.
- Coaching, guiding, and supporting the team so it can succeed at its assigned task and so management can be confident it is on track.
- Using the team's experience to deliver what the project intends in the marketplace and learn what it takes to make heavyweight teams work.

Leading Product Development

In essence, the project becomes a good demonstration to the organization of how effective heavyweight teams can be and what it takes to make them that way. There are four steps to accomplishing the above objectives.

Step 1: Create a process/approach for carrying out the tasks of detailed design and development that works for the heavyweight team.

This template defines for senior management, the team leader, the core team members, and the supporting organization how development under the team will proceed; it outlines a sequence of milestones the team will achieve that includes preparing a contract book and outlining the kinds and frequency of senior management reviews. This template will probably be modified as project work ensues, but it is an important first step in setting expectations for the team itself and providing a context for the rest of the organization to work with the heavyweight team.

Step 2: Define a project charter.

The charter defines the project's business purposes and specifies the product's desired market position and key performance objectives. The charter thus specifies the metrics that define product success and lays out the capabilities the team must develop. In its final form, the charter defines the mission of the project and the heavyweight team. When the project leader and the core team members agree to join this project, they commit themselves to delivering on the charter and being evaluated on the degree to which they do so.

Step 3: Select the team leader and the team, and draw up the contract book.

With both a process and a charter established, the people charged with carrying out the project must be chosen. The team must be cross-functional, and at least its core members should be co-located;

the leader should be appropriate to the team's mission. Because the intention is to demonstrate the power of the heavyweight team concept to the rest of the organization, the people who carry out this task must be up for it—they must be both qualified and committed. On the other hand, since the point is also to prove that the concept can be transferred, senior management should avoid populating the team with superheroes or company warhorses who can get things done no matter what the structure or process. Not only will the organization discount such an effort, but the team will not bring the right issues to the surface and teach the organization the right lessons.

Step 4: Support the team.

Behind this innocent phrase lies hard work. Creating a shared understanding in senior management and carrying out steps 1, 2, and 3 are all important elements of support. But in launching the team, the crucial issue is educating the key people within the functional groups and those who will be involved in support efforts. This education process evolves as the team begins to carry out its objectives. At the outset, the key functional people need to understand their new role, how their work needs to change (and will change) to support the team, and what issues will likely arise as the team's work unfolds. This must be more than exhortation. Many tasks the functions perform will be the same, but some will be different and some will be new. New skills and new attitudes are involved.

The team itself will also need significant educating and skills building. Team members may not know how to function as members of a heavyweight team, for example. They will need to learn how to work together and what being part of a core team—which has considerable authority and responsibility—implies. More than just working together, team members must learn to step back and examine the processes they are using—what works, what does not, and what needs to be changed. One principle we have learned over the years in our work with teams and in our research is that training and education must be part of the real work the team undertakes. Thus, we do not recommend seminars on team building divorced from what the team is actually doing. Rather, the team learns to operate as a team by working together on real problems.

All the ideas and concepts about the new role of senior management (described in Chapter 4) come into play during the process of implementing the heavyweight team. The team needs a sponsor/coach, for example, and considerable judgment about resources and support (an energy source) in order to accomplish its objectives.

Once the team is launched and operating, numerous issues will crop up as it seeks to carry out its work—and does so in ways that differ from established practice. The senior management sponsor must actively participate in negotiating the team's boundaries and identifying where it may responsibly challenge the status quo both to break new ground and to make progress. Thus, the sponsor works with the team and with senior management to review and evaluate the team's work and to advise the team.

As the project moves forward, the senior management group inevitably begins to encounter front-end issues. For example, when the team begins to experience success and builds momentum within the organization, the question of whether and when to launch a second heavyweight team may arise. Adding a second heavyweight team seriously complicates senior management's job, for all the issues attendant to planning and managing a portfolio of projects—not to mention determining the architecture that underlies them—come into play. Most senior management groups decide to wait until the first heavyweight team has completed its work before focusing on the front end of development and launching a second heavyweight team. This tack has the advantage of sustaining the first team's initiative through completion, thereby resulting in a thorough exploration and understanding of what that takes; it also has the effect of making the project highly visible and generating a strong impact.

Waiting for the first effort to finish, initiating a new team before it does so, or beginning the preplanning work associated with the left side of Figure 6–1 once the team is well on its way are all viable options. The key points are not to let the first team's momentum flag or withdraw support (intentionally or not) so that its significant efforts wither, and not to open the battle too soon on too many fronts (diluting management's attention and confusing the organization).

PITFALLS AND OBSTACLES There are two inherent sources of difficulty on the path above. The first is the relationship between the heavyweight team and the functions. Unless the team is completely self-sustaining and self-contained (which would make it an autonomous team), the functions are important to carrying out the work. But until the functional organizations learn how to reorient themselves—and provide the services to the team rather than making all the detailed decisions and doing all the work—there will probably be conflicts related to resource allocation, decision making about specific technical choices, and methods and procedures. Because these are natural conflicts in an organization that does not have experience with heavyweight teams, a development template or process that is laid out (step 1) at the outset, as well as educational support for the functional groups, are imperative.

The second difficulty involves the skills and capabilities of team members themselves. It is not a simple matter for people used to working within a functional organization—even within a lightweight team—to assume full responsibility for a project's success. It is not just becoming a "team member" that has to be learned; it's becoming this kind of a team member. New and different skills are needed, along with different attitudes and ways of making decisions and taking action. Moreover, team members participate in the team, but they also must provide leadership within their functions. Thus, they need to assume responsibility for a broad range of actions that they may also be required to execute.

Unless the organization currently has a number of people carrying out such demanding roles (in which case it probably has something akin to heavyweight teams already), the lack of the right skills and attitudes will create problems. For example, when Quantum, a disk-drive manufacturer with several hundred million dollars' worth of business annually, moved to heavyweight teams for platform projects, senior management did an audit and evaluation of people throughout the organization. It discovered among its several hundred employees only a handful with the skills needed to participate effectively as core members of a heavyweight team.

Because heavyweight teams demand a tough combination of skills and abilities—in terms of both depth and breadth—we strongly emphasize skills building, education, and significant support for team members as they undertake their project work. Without this effort, team members will fall back into their natural mode of functional representatives who meet together, but do not work together effectively as a team. On an ongoing basis, career paths as well as selection and training must be fundamentally altered so that qualified participants will be available when new teams are formed.

Path 2: Laying the Foundation through Architecture, the Funnel, and the Aggregate Project Plan

The second path to implementation concentrates on the planning processes in Figure 6–1. Like the first path, senior management is 100% on board. This path also has four broad steps, but there are important differences: in particular, there are fewer people, by and large, affected by the work initially, given the activities involved. That conclusion, however, depends on the nature of the business and how planning is carried out in general. Chapter 3 contains a thorough discussion of the specific activities involved in the first three steps; here we simply summarize them briefly.

Step 1: Create the product line architecture.

This is the key planning framework; on this path, it is the most effective starting point because it immediately brings to bear the planning and strategic skills senior management traditionally uses and establishes the key link between business strategy and the projects.

Step 2: Establish the funnel process.

With this step, senior management defines the process that takes ideas to projects based on the architecture and development capacity. This process also brings a language to the organization (enriched by the architecture discussions addressing project "types") that allows people in different functions to work together to develop effective plans and lay the foundation for effective execution.

Step 3: Draw up the aggregate project plan.

This will first involve assessing capacity and sizing up current and potential projects in light of resource constraints and opportunities. It then entails defining a portfolio of current and future projects that fit the capabilities and capacity and realize the product line architecture.

The three steps above are, of course, easy enough to describe; they are very, very difficult to carry out. The essential point is that the entire senior management team must be engaged in these three steps. Senior management is basically responsible for creating three "deliverables": the architecture, the funnel, and the aggregate project plan. These will perforce apply to the business at a particular point in time given the information on hand. However, once these three mechanisms have been established, senior management steps back and evaluates what has been accomplished so as to make the activities on the left-hand side more than one-time events. With that evaluation in hand, senior management can take the fourth step.

Step 4: Create the front-end process.

Having created the three mechanisms above, senior management is ready to define the process for doing this work regularly. The first three steps are likely to uncover significant gaps in information and reveal major ways of improving the work. Simply working together on the difficult assignment of creating the architecture, funnel, and aggregate project plan generates new insights into how to do business. These have to be dealt with and taken advantage of, and senior management needs to determine how these insights will be incorporated into the ongoing planning effort.

The temptation might be, at this point, to move immediately to issues of execution and begin launching heavyweight teams. We have discovered, however, that senior management needs more than one iteration of the four steps before shifting its attention to creating new kinds of teams. The planning process needs to be sustainable, repeatable, and resilient (i.e., able to be changed frequently without falling apart). It needs to be done two or three times (on a two- to three-month cycle) to verify performance, establish good practices, and build momentum.

PITFALLS AND OBSTACLES The difficulties encountered in taking the path focused on preproject planning are different from those found on the path that focuses on project execution through heavyweight teams. The first is, simply, a lack of information. This is particularly difficult when creating the APP, because digging into the issues of portfolio management and capacity matching requires extensive information about resources and resource availability. Applying a rigorous, systematic analysis is critical and requires more and better information than most firms are used to compiling. Without this information, senior managers can only draw up approximations, and so will have difficulty establishing their credibility with the rest of the organization and enforcing discipline on themselves. For the funnel, information is also critical. An important starting point is to understand current practice and the organization's "natural" tendencies, and this is often difficult to do.

A second major impediment, even more serious than lack of information, is the attitudes of senior managers themselves. While these can assume many forms, they reflect, by and large, the fact that most senior managers got where they are by being good at the old system. Thus, a serious obstacle to progress on this second implementation path appears when senior managers' instincts, skills, and identities as effective managers lead them to do precisely the wrong thing in seeking to implement the ideas we recommend.

To be the chief architect of the product line, senior managers must assume a role that in many organizations has been delegated to a staff group. We have worked with organizations in which the following scenario—odd as it may appear—is almost a daily occurrence. The senior management group gets together and reviews market opportunities, new technologies under development, and competitors' moves. The discussion is at a relatively high level and observers are puzzled when questions that seem straightforward (yet require some depth of analysis or specific pieces of data) are deferred for future consideration or referred to staffers. Later, we discover that it is considered a badge of honor among senior managers *not* to be caught up in (bothered by) details, but to operate solely at a very high level of abstract analysis. Characteristic of such meetings is the complete absence of materials on the conference table save notepads—used for elaborate doodles. To be a chief architect, of course, means getting into, and being responsible for, precisely those details that are essential to making crucial decisions about the business' future. Getting at the right level of detail is, of course, important. But doing good architecture from 30,000 feet is virtually impossible.

Another factor that can obstruct progress on this path is the unwillingness or inability of senior managers to make really hard choices. Establishing the APP, for example, requires a focused effort and attention to the critical few things the organization is commited to. As we've noted, this entails that senior managers who firmly defend the "more is more" idea instead adopt the "less is more" dictum. This requires discipline and consistency. Many senior managers have gotten to their positions by constantly pushing, prodding, and coaxing the organization to produce more and more by putting more and more on its plate. This is what we called the illusion of activity in Chapter 1. It is dangerous and a true impediment to effective and efficient product development. Senior managers must not only come to believe this, but act in a manner that demonstrates this belief.

Both these barriers underscore the importance of creating a shared understanding in the senior management team—100% commitment—*whether path 1 or path 2 is chosen.* Everyone on the senior management team must understand the fundamental principles behind a new approach to product development and their implications for senior management's role. Ideally, all senior managers will exhibit the kind of flexibility and adaptability required to move from the traditional functional setup to the more effective team-oriented approach; to move from the fragmented, confusing, minimalist planning "structure" to one that is more focused, streamlined, and substantive. In practice this is not always the case, and senior executives must assume responsibility for getting people in their organization and on the senior management team with the attitudes and skills for success.

Choosing Path 1 or Path 2

While both paths will eventually get the business to a comprehensive system, each is appropriate in different circumstances. We will lay out some considerations senior managers need to address in selecting one over the other.

WHY PATH 1? This path, with its emphasis on creating a heavyweight team as a "demonstration" project, is more appropriate where the business has a reasonable front-end planning process yet faces significant pressure in the marketplace, particularly for platform projects. So, for example, Ford in the 1980s faced enormous competitive pressure regarding lead time, engineering productivity, and product quality—it had to bring to market much better products, quickly, while using fewer resources than in the past. However, for many years Ford had been conducting "cycle planning," whereby it examined its project portfolio and the resources available, and attempted to match programs with resources. Ford also had a product architecture in place.

In retrospect, it was clear that many things about the planning process needed improvement, but Ford did not face a situation in which it had grossly overloaded its development system, had a lot of projects going on that it was unaware of, or was confused about basic objectives. Thus, it made sense to focus on the right-side path. In short, Ford's planning foundation was reasonable, if not excellent, and the real issues involved execution. Thus, it embarked on a long process of improving the template of its development process and implementing heavyweight teams. As the team's and Ford's performance in execution improved, issues in planning and strategy came to the fore because those issues had begun to constrain individual teams. Addressing the issues moved Ford toward a more comprehensive, coherent approach.

WHY PATH 2? The choice of the planning path is well illustrated by a company we shall call PreQuip, a manufacturer of medical instruments. In the late 1980s, PreQuip's senior management was frustrated by a lack of development productivity. It had many projects under way, but nothing seemed to get finished (at least, not in a reasonable amount of time); the system was significantly overloaded, creating the congestion and problems we have alluded to throughout this book. Moreover, there was significant confusion and a lack of consensus between senior management and the functions about where the company was headed. In these circumstances, implementing heavyweight teams would have failed. The senior management group might have been masterful at implementing teams, but the teams would have floundered given the confusion, overloading of resources, and general congestion throughout the organization.

Thus, it made good sense to start with the second path. This was hardly an easy task, as senior managers had to confront the fact that they themselves had initiated many of the (uncompleted) projects in place. They had to create a product line architecture that would force them to think through, deeply and thoroughly, where they were taking the business. They also had to face the fact that they did not have the capacity to do everything everybody could think of. They had to get from more is more to less is more. The result was a long process whereby senior management came to grips with the realities and limitations of the organization's capacity, given the economics of the business and in spite of what appeared to be an endless stream of competitively necessary projects.

They ended up reformulating, reshaping, and dramatically reducing the number of initiatives under way at any one time. An architecture and an APP gave senior management a much tighter focus and also established clear objectives for the business as a whole. At that point they were ready for heavyweight teams. Had they tried that first, however, without the planning foundation, they would have gotten nowhere.

WHY NOT BOTH AT ONCE? Since the goal is to have a development process with a strong foundation of planning and excellent execution, the obvious question is why not do both at once? Our immediate answer is that it is very hard (if not impossible) to do. Yet, there are circumstances in which it is possible to pursue both. In general, if the enterprise is relatively small, so that the job of communicating and educating is not a major undertaking, it is possible to do both at once, successfully. Also, if the product line itself is relatively simple (so planning is not a major undertaking), the pursuit of both may be warranted.

Thus, in Chapter 5, we saw a fusing of planning and execution as the team charged with the FunSaver project execution played a central role in planning the product line under the direction of senior management. Indeed, before the FunSaver, there was no product line. In that sense, the project was the business. However, when we look at the single-use business in its total context, we see the crucial role of senior management leadership in implementation. Thus, attempts to get into the single-use business when the unit was under the film group went nowhere: they were snarled in a very complex situation with strong conflicts about resources and fears of cannibalization with existing product lines. These circumstances severely threatened and limited the viability of either path. It wasn't until senior management moved the project that it could go forward.

In effect, Kodak cleared out the underbrush and opened up the field to allow the FunSaver team to operate effectively. Once the team got into action, it was able to learn from its experience in the market and to reformulate the architecture and reestablish the planning process. In that sense, it was working from both the left and the right sides of our attention-influence diagram. In essence, the initial set of projects was the only game in town for those involved. They could see clearly the value of following both the planning and the team path concurrently, and had the support and energy needed to do so.

What matters most is that the organization focus on those opportunities of most value, given the constraints it faces. Where existing planning work poses a significant—insurmountable—barrier to progress through teams, senior management must address the foundation work on the left side. Where that congestion is not present and planning processes, architecture, and capacity management are adequate, then teams are an effective starting point. *In the end, both the left and right sides will be modified as a result of the effort involved in starting at either end.*

The implication, therefore, is that the decision to take one or the other path, or to attempt both at once, depends on senior management's assessment of where the business currently stands. What problems are to be solved? Is the development system overloaded? Does the business have a product line architecture and an effective strategy in place? What does the development system look like? Realistically, can the organization currently support heavyweight teams? How can ideas be turned into projects that make it to the marketplace with the results expected?

Only by honestly asking—and answering—these questions can the senior management team achieve successful implementation.

Leading the Implementation Journey

No matter what path senior management chooses to pursue, the journey toward a new approach to development and a new pattern of senior management leadership has all the earmarks of a major development project. Framed in these terms, each path of implementation has a rhythm, a set of milestones, and phases of development. And senior management is the core team that plans and executes the journey.

There is, therefore, wonderful symmetry in senior management's new role in product development and in implementing the new pattern and approach. As the core implementation team, senior management must practice what it preaches. It must establish the model for how planning should be done, how processes should work, and how teams should operate. Making implementation a project and making senior management the core heavyweight team means that senior management must lead by taking action. Below, we lay out the basic phases, milestones, and core team actions in implementation.

Phase I: Assess and Align

In this phase, senior management, as a team, assesses the situation regarding the current state of planning and execution in development. It examines the planning process and the project portfolio; it reviews the product line architecture and its fit with business strategy; it determines what the development funnel actually looks like; it looks at how it approachs teams and teamwork. It addresses the functional groups and their role—explicit and implicit—in the organization. And it honestly looks in the mirror and assesses its own role in all these processes.

Accompanying this assessment is a discussion of the fundamental objectives and principles senior management intends to use in improving product development. The whole focus of this effort is to align senior management in its understanding of the problem, its objectives in solving it, and the path it intends to follow.

Milestone 1: Implementation Concept

The outcome of phase I, and thus senior management's first major milestone, is the creation of an implementation concept. This in-

Leading Product Development

cludes choosing a path, designating the sequence of steps the senior management team proposes to take, and identifying the key tasks to be accomplished. Furthermore, it indicates the basis on which this effort will be judged—how success will be recognized.

Phase II: Initial Launch

In this phase, the senior management team launches its initial activities (following the paths outlined above). If it pursues the teams strategy, it launches the first heavyweight team; for the planning path, it initiates work on the product line architecture, the funnel, and the APP. This culminates in milestone 2.

Milestone 2: Liftoff

The issue here is, "Do we have liftoff?" Is the first step working? Clearly, this milestone has to be planned so that sufficient time passes for senior management to reliably and confidently evaluate project performance to date. It must determine whether progress is sufficient to build momentum and whether the project has escaped (or is in the process of escaping) the gravity of the old order.

Phase III: Expand the Effort

In this phase, senior management must move beyond the initial set of activities. There is a choice. One option is to decide how to move forward along the path defined by the initial steps. Thus, if the right-side path has been chosen, the question is, "How do we take our effort on the heavyweight teams forward and expand it?" This might involve implementing learning acquired thus far about how functions work; it might involve revising selection criteria or more training of team members; or it might entail developing tools and methods that would help teams function effectively. Or the decision might be to launch a second team to build on the experiences of the first.

If the left-side path was chosen, senior management must determine if it has completed a sufficient number of cycles of planning so that the APP and the architecture are working in synch and the funnel process is up and running. The senior management team may need to provide additional information, create a new process, or change the existing planning process elsewhere in the organization to solidify the effort. The issue then becomes whether to move to the other path (i.e., begin to establish heavyweight teams) or whether something else is needed. (This is about the time to make that move; senior managers must avoid the temptation of endlessly refining the planning procedures but never actually implementing them via teams.)

Milestone 3: Building Capability

The issue in passing this milestone is whether, in fact, the senior management group has been able to expand the effort beyond the initial set of activities. The point here is that the paths begin to converge. Those beginning with teams would not only have launched a second team, they would be initiating the first steps in the planning process (e.g., product line architecture). Those who began with planning would have gone through several planning cycles, and now would be launching the first heavyweight team. The idea is that the effort has expanded, development "energy" is being created, and the total, comprehensive approach—one development path—is in sight.

Phase IV: Solidifying the Effort

In this phase, the project begins to deepen the change within the organization, improving how teams operate and how the planning process works, and solving problems that have emerged in adapting to the changing circumstances triggered by the marketplace, evolving technology, and competition. The objective of this phase is to make the new approach to development planning and execution a natural part of the business. This is, in effect, institutionalization through ongoing improvement.

Milestone 4: Second Nature

The project passes this milestone when the new approach has really taken hold. Senior management has launched the project, achieved liftoff, and built capability—but have attitudes changed? Is it really second nature to work this way? A test is to consider returning to the old approach. Does it seem uncomfortable? Difficult? Downright old-fashioned, not to mention horribly inefficient? If that is the case, then the new approach has made its mark. There is neither incentive nor interest in returning to the past.

Finally, as part of the effort to ensure that the new approach becomes second nature, senior management ensures that it is a living system. Senior managers are constantly reviewing, evaluating, adjusting, and adapting to changing circumstances. Because it is now second nature to do this, senior managers are rewarded not just by the consistent performance of their development process but by the awareness that they created, shaped, and developed the process. They have not been mere caretakers or clerks, but architects and leaders.

Creating the Attitudes and Behaviors of Leaders

Thus far, our focus has been on the processes and structures that can be used to implement a new development process. These are crucial in giving senior managers the traction they need to make progress. But to make the process really work and the system come alive, senior managers need to make personal changes in their attitudes and behavior. It is these personal changes that will provide energy and enable individuals to accept, support, and enthusiastically embrace the new ways of development. In fact, the potential obstacles identified in paths 1 and 2 represent failures to achieve the required personal changes.

Our studies have identified half a dozen dimensions of personal change critical to implementation. While other dimensions may also come into play, these six personal themes provide a solid foundation for success in implementing new processes and structures. Addressing the following six dimensions creates and fosters the attitudes and behavior that enable development leadership.

1. *Balancing function and product to achieve an integrated business process.* Depth of expertise in individual functions as well as breadth of understanding across functions, customers, and markets are critical to outstanding product development. To succeed, product development must be an integrated business process. To lead that process, senior managers need to value and nurture expertise, balance it against the requirements of the product, and see everything from the perspective of the business as a whole.

2. *Rigorous, systematic, and objective analysis of development proposals.* While the need for such methodology in approving new projects is obvious, it's equally important as a basis for capacity and portfolio planning, milestone reviews, and resolving cross-functional issues in a specific project. Such analyses must replace politics, power, and status as the basis of decision making.

3. *Increased emphasis on identifying, addressing, and changing patterns.* Development is a setting where all too often each issue is viewed as unique, requiring a unique solution. Yet management exercises its greatest leverage by working on patterns and their causes. Striving to solve only the specific problem—behavior typical of the right-hand side of the attention-influence diagram—must give way to striving to eliminate the causes of such problems.

4. *Instilling discipline into commitments.* Organizations work best when agreed-upon plans and commitments are adhered to and can be relied on. Whether it is in allocating resources, setting schedules, or agreeing to outcomes, discipline and follow-through bring added power, efficiency, and effectiveness to all aspects of development.

5. *Improvement as a journey, not an event.* Building on the idea of patterns, every effort to solve a development issue or eliminate a problem must also be viewed as an opportunity to improve the process and build capability. Continually strengthening the foundation—of skills, tools, procedures, and attitudes—will make future improvements easier and quicken their pace.

6. *Behavior and action reflect true values, attitudes, and beliefs.* Senior managers reveal their real attitudes and values by what they do. To lead product development, senior managers must behave in a manner consistent with the values and principles that have been agreed to, accepted, and reinforced across the organization. Otherwise, they may profess to lead, but no one will follow. Indeed, people in the organization will quickly spot the inconsistency, discern the true values of senior management (what it "really cares about"), and act accordingly.

These six themes provide senior management with a way to gauge its own behavior in implementation. Periodically, members of the senior management team should step back and ask themselves—both as a team and as individuals—hard questions: "Are we treating development as a business process? Do we practice what we preach? Are we disciplined in our commitments? Are we rigorous, systematic, and objective in our work? Are we going after root causes and changing patterns?" But the only way such questions (and answers) will have an impact is if senior management addresses them explicitly. The need for and the importance of these attitudes must be communicated at the outset, ways to achieve them planned, and success reinforced.

Action along these lines is crucial. Simply put, when it comes to leading product development, change begins at home. Senior management sets the pattern. It teaches the organization the new ways of planning by the way it plans. It shows what teams are like and what teamwork means by the way it works together as a team. But there is more. Senior management provides not only the model, but the motivation for change. People in the organization look to senior management to determine what, if anything, has changed, and whether it is likely to stay changed. They may listen and defer to the practices of the moment, but until they think they are real and lasting, they won't buy in.

This is the challenge. Senior management must first change itself individually, then as a team, and then go to work on others.

Leadership and Leaders*

We began this book with the recognition that constantly creating great products is difficult but powerful. To use a mountain climbing analogy, the path is not easy, the climb is steep, but the view is breathtaking and very few can follow those who make it. Without in any way slighting the role of good, sturdy hiking boots, strong ropes, or a good backpack, we have emphasized the importance of leaders who know how to pick the right mountain, chart the course, build climbing skills, and lead the business so that projects overcome obstacles and achieve key objectives on the trail to the top.

---

*This section is taken from "Make Projects the School for Leaders" (H. K. Bowen, K. B. Clark, C. A. Holloway, and S. C. Wheelwright, *Harvard Business Review,* September-October 1994, pp. 138–140).

Leading Product Development

We are now beginning to understand what effective leadership of development implies and how it can be achieved. The tools and mechanisms—product line architecture, the funnel, the aggregate project plan, charters, contracts, and heavyweight teams—and the new roles for senior management have proven powerful in understanding what leadership means and in putting leadership into action.

Invariably, however, senior executives arrive at this point with some fundamental questions: "What we've seen here makes sense. But look at what you are asking these heavyweight team and business leaders to do. You want them to be influential across a range of disciplines. Yet they have to be able to integrate and see the whole. You want them to have a down-to-earth business sense. Yet they need imagination: their crystal ball must anticipate customers' unarticulated needs, preempt competitors' moves, and spot technological trends. It's not that we don't have any people like them, but where are we going to find enough of them?"

The problem is challenging. Companies need project leaders not only of substantial quality, but who can serve as team members and lead the effort within their respective functions. What is more, they need senior managers (heads of businesses and of functions) capable of a very different kind of leadership than they've exercised in the past.

The challenge is both to find and develop the right kind of people and to expand significantly their capacity for leadership. The challenge is to understand what leadership requires of people and to create a process and a system in which leaders develop naturally as part of the life of the business. In the companies we have studied where leadership thrives, senior managers consistently do three things.

1. *They expect leadership.* Leaders will not and cannot lead unless that role has been defined and that expectation established. Part of

this involves simply setting up something like a heavyweight structure (or a dedicated team) with formal roles for the project leader and the core functional leaders. But it also means setting expectations for what senior management wants those leaders to do. Expectations define not only the responsibilities but also the attitudes, behavior, and patterns of action required to carry them out.

2. *They support leaders.* In some of the leading product development companies we've studied, the job or project was not an attractive assignment. One engineering manager at Digital Equipment Corporation, for example, spoke disdainfully about his role as a project leader. "It's not my real job," he said. He derived satisfaction and respect only from his engineering work and his role as an engineering manager. In such settings, project leaders are little more than clerks. So part of what support means is to redefine the status of the role.

Leaders also need supporting processes and systems that give them what they need to lead. They need the concept of a product line architecture to provide a context and to guide their decisions about individual products and their relationship to the product line. They need information on development capacity and the discipline of an aggregate project plan. They need heavyweight teams with charters that define the link between the project and the business strategy. They need a contract that defines the boundaries of projects, their vision, their objectives, and their access to resources. They need meaningful control and influence over critical resources. They need a license to challenge what needs to be challenged for development to achieve its objectives. And, above all else, they need an organization that gives them the right experience, training, and personal development. This is what the outstanding companies do.

3. *They reward leaders.* To be consistent, companies have to reward good leaders for substance—actions taken and results

achieved—not just form. There is much to learn here from the small, hungry entrepreneurial companies, in which the rewards for leading development and for building the business are clear. The coin of the realm is equity, promotion, and the chance to take on the next really great project. Too often, big companies offer too few rewards. Especially where the functions control the rewards, leading a project can be a big negative—out of sight, out of mind. It is almost impossible to attract the best people to project leadership if the job is not valued or means missed promotions or lower compensation. Outstanding companies value and reward development leadership.

Taken together, these actions and the tools and mechanisms defined in Chapter 2 define a distinctive pattern of senior management leadership in product development. At its heart is the notion that the way to grow and attract leaders and make them effective is to make projects the engines that power the enterprise. In most companies, but especially those with a strong functional orientation, projects are too often an exception to the standard way of getting things done. The functions are at the center of the business.

But to architect the product, to build a development portfolio, to make heavyweight teams work, and to build great leaders capable of creating great products, projects must be central. Indeed, in organizations where the concept of teams and leadership takes hold, projects become the way the business gets anything complex and significant done on time, on target, and on budget. And we mean anything: entering a new market, opening a new store, building a new information system, starting up a new channel of distribution, or introducing a new class of service. Anything that is complex, confronts an uncertain future, involves multiple functions or disciplines, and must happen under rigorous time, budget, and quality constraints is a target of opportunity for a heavyweight or dedicated team and heavyweight leadership.

It should be clear from this perspective that where projects are central and leaders thrive, the values, concepts, and practices we have laid out permeate the organization. In an important way, leadership in product development and leadership in carrying out major projects is like a fractal: no matter how far down in the organization one goes, one sees the same pattern.

Once that happens, the question the senior executive posed earlier—where to find enough leaders—finds a ready answer. As that pattern of getting work done and that kind of leadership begin to take hold, experience in the business attracts and creates a new kind of leader. Not everyone will be a leader, but leaders will emerge naturally as part of normal growth and development within the firm. Leading projects will become the way one develops as a manager. Over time, the ranks of senior management will be filled by people capable of integrative leadership with a rich background of getting things done through projects. For them, building capabilities, using projects to change the company, and fostering leadership throughout the organization will be second nature. And it is that capacity that will be crucial in the turbulent years ahead. It is the capacity for perpetually renewing the enterprise—the ability to see a different future, to seize opportunities, to marshal resources, and to take action to build that future—that will be the touchstone of the future. And the trek up the mountain will be led by those with perspective, imagination, and the capacity for action.

Additional Readings

Chapter 1—The Leadership Challenge

For a further discussion of competition and new product development capability, see Steven C. Wheelwright and Kim B. Clark, *Revolutionizing Product Development* (New York: Free Press, 1992), chapter 1; see also Steven C. Wheelwright and Kim B. Clark, "Competing Through Development Capability in a Manufacturing-Based Organization," *Business Horizons* 35(4), 1992, pp. 29–43.

For additional information on Hewlett-Packard and the development of the DeskJet, see H. Kent Bowen, Kim B. Clark, Charles A. Holloway, and Steven C. Wheelwright, eds., *The Perpetual Enterprise Machine: Seven Keys to Corporate Renewal through Successful Product and Process Development* (New York: Oxford University Press, 1994), chapter 14; for a discussion of the experience of the Vancouver plant in making broad improvements in manufacturing, see Robert H. Hayes, Steven C. Wheelwright, and Kim B. Clark, *Dynamic Manufacturing* (New York: Free Press, 1988), chapter 12; for a discussion of senior management's role in the DeskJet project, see H. Kent Bowen, Kim B. Clark, Charles A. Holloway, and Steven C. Wheelwright, "Make Projects the School for Leaders," *Harvard Business Review*, September-October 1994, pp. 131–140.

Many authors have examined the issues of product development and innovation in recent years. Among them are: Willard I. Zangwill, *Lightning Strategies for Innovation: How the World's Best Firms Create New Products* (New York: Lexington Books, 1993); Christopher Meyer, *Fast Cycle Time: How to Align Purpose, Strategy, and Structure for Speed* (New York: Free Press, 1993); and Preston G. Smith and Donald G. Reinertsen, *Developing Products in Half the Time* (New York: Van Nostrand Reinhold, 1991).

Chapter 2—A New Role for Senior Management: From Problem to Solution

For further discussion of the attention/influence index, see Robert H. Hayes, Steven C. Wheelwright, and Kim B. Clark, *Dynamic Manufacturing* (New York: Free Press, 1988), chapter 10; and Steven C. Wheelwright and Kim B. Clark, *Revolutionizing Product Development* (New York: Free Press, 1992), chapter 2. A classic (and still timely) piece on senior management's role is F.W. Gluck and R.N. Foster, "Managing Technological Change: A Box of Cigars for Brad," *Harvard Business Review*, September–October 1975, pp. 139–150.

Chapter 3—Less Is More: Building an Effective Project Portfolio

For additional background on the concepts developed here, see Steven C. Wheelwright and Kim B. Clark, *Revolutionizing Product Development* (New York: Free Press, 1992), chapters 3–6.

For an example of managing project portfolios in the worldwide auto industry, see Michael D. Watkins and Kim B. Clark, "Strategies for Managing a Project Portfolio" (Harvard Business School Working Paper 93–004); see also Steven C. Wheelwright and Kim B. Clark, "Creating Project Plans to Focus Product Development," *Harvard Business Review*, March–April 1992, pp. 20–32.

For a discussion of maps and mapping, see Robert H. Hayes, Steven C. Wheelwright, and Kim B. Clark, *Dynamic Manufacturing* (New York: Free Press, 1988), chapter 10; see also Steven C. Wheelwright and W. Earl Sasser, Jr., "The New Product Development Map," *Harvard Business Review*, May–June 1989, pp. 112–125.

For a discussion of the development funnel, see Hayes, Wheelwright, and Clark, *Dynamic Manufacturing*, chapter 10. For related discussions of milestones, phases, and review processes, see Michael E. McGrath, Michael T. Anthony, and Amram R. Shapiro, *Product Development: Success through Product and Cycle-Time Excellence* (Boston: Butterworth-Heinemann, 1992); and Robert G. Cooper, "Third-Generation New Product Processes," *Journal of Product Innovation* 11(1), January 1994, pp. 3–14.

For a review of the literature on project selection and R&D, see M. L. Liberatore and G. J. Titus, "The Practice of Management Science in R&D Project Management," *Management Science* 29(8), August 1983, pp. 962–974; Muhittin Oral, Ossama Kettani, and Pascal Lang, "A Methodology for Collective Evaluation and Selection of Industrial R&D Projects," *Management Science* 37(7), July 1991, pp. 871–885; Albert H. Rubinstein, *Managing Technology in the Decentralized Firm* (New York: John Wiley and Sons, 1989), chapter 7; Edward B. Roberts, "What We've Learned: Managing Invention and Innovation," *Research-Technology Management 31(1)*, January–February 1988, pp. 11–29; and Norman R. Baker, Stephen G. Green, and Alden S. Bean, "How Management Can Influence the Generation of Ideas," *Research Management* 28(6), November-December 1985, pp. 35–42.

Chapter 4—Creating Consistently Effective Project Teams

The literature on teams is extensive. For additional reading, see Steven C. Wheelwright and Kim B. Clark, *Revolutionizing Product Development* (New York: Free Press, 1992), chapter 8; Gloria Barczak and David Wilemon, "Leadership Differences in New Product Development Teams," *Journal of Product Innovation Management* 6, 1989, pp. 259–267. See also Kim B. Clark and Takahiro Fujimoto, *Product Development Performance* (Boston: Harvard Business School, 1991), chapter 9; Kim B. Clark and Steven C. Wheelwright, "Organizing and Leading 'Heavyweight' Development Teams," *California Management Review* 34 (3), Summer 1992, pp. 9–28; Christopher Meyer, *Fast Cycle Time: How to Align Purpose, Strategy and Structure for Speed* (New York: Free Press, 1993); J. R. Katzenbach and D. K. Smith, *Creating the High-Performance Organization* (Boston: Harvard Business School Press, 1992); and H. Kent Bowen, Kim B. Clark, Charles A. Holloway, and Steven C. Wheelwright, eds., *The Perpetual Enterprise Machine: Seven Keys to Corporate Renewal through Successful Product and Process Development* (New York: Oxford University Press, 1994), chapter 5.

Chapter 5—Leadership in Action: Developing Single-Use Cameras at Kodak

For additional background on Kodak and the development of the FunSaver, see H. Kent Bowen, Kim B. Clark, Charles A. Holloway, and Steven C. Wheelwright, eds., *The Perpetual Enterprise Machine: Seven Keys to Corporate Renewal through Successful Product and Process Development* (New York: Oxford University Press, 1994), chapter 12; and Al Van der Moere, "The Kodak FunSaver Story," Boston University School of Management Manufacturing Roundtable Seminar, March 20, 1991. The FunSaver development project has been well-documented in the popular press; much of the information for this chapter has been acquired from publicly available sources, as well as from presentations by Eastman Kodak Company management.

Chapter 6—Turning Promise into Reality

For general background on organizational change, see Michael Beer, Russell A. Eisenstat, and Bert Spector, *The Critical Path to Corporate Renewal* (Boston: Harvard Business School Press, 1990) and the references therein. See also Dorothy Leonard-Barton, "Implementation as Mutual Adaptation of Technology and Organization," *Research Policy* 17, 1988, pp. 251–267; and John Hendry and Gerry Johnson, with Julia Newton, eds., *Strategic Thinking: Leadership and the Management of Change* (New York: John Wiley & Sons, 1993).

Index

Activity, illusion of, 7
Aggregate project plan (APP)
  benefits of, 63–65
  defining the project set, 60–61
  implementation stage and creation
    of, 145–46
  matching projects to capability
    and capacity, 61
  pitfalls and obstacles for, 146–49
  revisiting, 62–63
Amalgamated Inc., Spectrometer
    Division, case example, 23–28,
    30–32
Apple Macintosh
  platform projects of, 56–57
  product generation map example,
    53–54
Architecting the product line, 53–55,
    58–59
Assessment and alignment (Phase I),
    153
Attitudes of senior management,
    implementation and creating,
    156–59

Autonomous team structure
  advantages and disadvantages of,
    85, 86
  description of, 84
  energy source and, 93
  selecting members for, 87

Back-end leadership roles, 39–41
Behaviors of senior management,
    implementation and creating,
    156–59
Board of directors, role of, 42–45
Braun, 96
Breakthrough products, 52
Business Week, 13

Capability and capacity, matching
    projects to, 61
Capability building (Milestone 3), 155
Case examples
  See also Eastman Kodak, FunSaver
    project at
  Amalgamated Inc., Spectrometer
    Division, 23–28, 30–32

Index

Case examples *(cont.)*
  Chaparral Steel, 88–89
  Global Electronics' compact disc
    projects, 8–12
  Hewlett-Packard's DeskJet
    printer project, 15–19
  Pilkington Barnes-Hind, 69–71
  PreQuip, 150–51
  Rubbermaid, 13, 14
Chaparral Steel, teams at, 88–89
Coca-Cola, platform projects of, 58
Commitment manager, teamwork and
    senior manager's role, 95–97
Commitment manager leadership
    role, 40
Competition, pressure of responding
    to, 6–7
Contract book, creating the, 91–92,
    140–41
Cross-functional teamwork, example
    of, 111–19, 130

Decision making, negative conse-
    quences of avoiding, 61–62
Derivative products, 52
Development funnel
  factors that affect, 67–69
  idea generation, 66
  idea merging into a single project,
    66–67
  idea testing and evaluation, 66
  implementation stage and creation
    of, 145
  pitfalls and obstacles for, 146–49
  resources and commitments
    applied, 67
  role of, 65–66
  steps and example for creating,
    69–71
Digital Equipment Corp., 161
Direction setter leadership role
  description of, 37
  tasks and objectives of, 48–49

Direction setting
  in Amalgamated Inc. case example,
    30
  role of, 28–29

Eastman Kodak, functional team
    structure at, 84–85
Eastman Kodak, FunSaver project at
  background of, 104–108
  CAD/CAM system, use of, 113,
    128, 130
  creation of the Weekend, 113–14
  cross-functional teamwork and
    development of, 111–19,
    130
  derivative products from, 105,
    121–22
  Flash model, 122, 123
  heavyweight team structure at,
    116, 129–30
  how competition from Fuji was
    handled, 107, 108–11, 128
  how problems with FunSaver II
    were met, 122–27
  importance of timing, 129
  manufacturing acceptance process
    (MAP) of, 106
  manufacturing role, 130–31
  next generation of, 119, 121–22
  organizational structure and
    challenges facing Kodak, 105–7
  panoramic model, 108, 112
  promotion of derivatives, 115
  recycling issues, 121
  senior management's role,
    118–19, 129
  success of, 119, 121
  summation of, 127–33
  types of problems confronted by
    Kodak, 131–32
Effort
  expansion of (Phase III), 154–55
  solidifying (Phase IV), 155–56

Employees, selecting, training and
    developing, 29
  in Amalgamated Inc. case example,
    30–32
  importance of, 29
Energy source
  leadership role, 39–40
  senior management's role with,
    92–95
  team structure and, 93–94
Envisioning
  in Amalgamated Inc. case example,
    30
  role of, 28–29, 30

Ford Motor Co., 149–50
Fortune, 13, 14
Front-end leadership roles, 37–39
Front-end process, implementation
    stage and creation of, 146
Fuji
  PhotoFilm, 107
  QuickSnap, 107, 108, 128
  QuickSnap Flash, 119
Functional team structure
  advantages and disadvantages of,
    84–85
  description of, 83
  energy source and, 93
  selecting members for, 87
Funnel. *See* Development funnel

Goal establishment, team launchers
    and, 90
Global Electronics
  compact disc projects, case
    example, 8–12
  team structure at, 83
Graphing plans, benefits of, 63, 64

Heavyweight team structure
  advantages and disadvantages of,
    85, 86

description of, 84
energy source and, 93–94
implementing heavyweight teams
    (Path 1), 139–44
pitfalls and obstacles, 143–44
selecting members for, 87
Hewlett-Packard
  DeskJet printer project, 15–19
  project portfolio of, 72

Idea
  factors that affect, 67–69
  generation, 66
  merging into a single project,
    66–67
  resources and commitments
    applied, 67
  testing and evaluation, 66
Implementation concept (Milestone
    1), 153–54
Implementation framework
  assessment and alignment (Phase
    I), 153
  capability building (Milestone 3),
    155
  choosing between Path 1 or Path
    2, 149–52
  creating the attitudes and behaviors
    of leaders, 156–59
  defining the improvement path,
    138–52
  expansion of effort (Phase III),
    154–55
  implementation concept
    (Milestone 1), 153–54
  implementing heavyweight teams
    (Path 1), 139–44
  initial launch (Phase II), 154
  laying the foundation (Path 2),
    144–49
  leading the implementation
    journey, 152–56
  liftoff (Milestone 2), 154

Index

Implementation framework *(cont.)*
pitfalls and obstacles for Path 1,
143–44
  pitfalls and obstacles for Path 2,
  146–49
  second nature (Milestone 4),
  156
  solidifying the effort (Phase IV),
  155–56
  steps in, 136–37
Initial launch (Phase II), 154
Intel, 1, 2

Leadership
  See also Senior management
  description of effective, 45–46
  expectation of, 160–61
  importance of, 1–2, 159–63
  rewarding, 161–62
  role of senior management, 2–3
  support of, 161
Leadership roles
  back-end, 39–41
  commitment manager, 40
  direction setter, 37, 48–49
  energy source, 39–40
  front-end, 37–39
  portfolio manager, 38, 59–65
  process creator/owner, 39, 65–69
  process improver, 41, 98–100
  product line architect, 37–38,
  50–55, 58–59
  sponsor/coach, 40–41
  team launcher, 39
Learning, process improver and,
  98–100
Liftoff (Milestone 2), 154
Lightweight team structure
  advantages and disadvantages of,
  85–86
  description of, 83–84
  energy source and, 93
  selecting members for, 87

Performance, process improver and,
  98–100
Pilkington Barnes-Hind, 69–71
Platform products
  definition of, 52
  examples of, 56–58
Portfolio manager leadership role
  description of, 38
  tasks and objectives of, 59–65
Position, product generation map
  and, 54–55
PreQuip, 150–51
Process approach, creating a, 140
Process creator/owner leadership
  role
  description of, 39
  tasks and objectives of, 65–69
Process improver leadership role, 41,
  98–100
Product development
  effects of, on the whole business,
  5–6
  importance of consistent, 2–3
  responding to competition, 6–7
  timing of management involvement and influence on, 21–23
  uncertainty and, 6
  views of senior management
  when product development is
  not considered critical, 3–5
Product generation map
  Apple Macintosh example, 53–54
  position and, 54–55
  relationships and, 55
  timing and, 55
  type and, 55
Product line architect
  definition of, 50
  implementation stage and creation
  of, 145
  pitfalls and obstacles for, 146–49
Product line architect leadership role
  advantages of, 58–59

architecting the product line,
53–55, 58–59
defining product types, 51–53
description of, 37–38
tasks and objectives of, 50–55, 58–59
Product relationships, product
generation map and, 55
Products, types of
breakthrough, 52
derivative, 52
platform, 52, 56–58
product generation map and, 55
support, 52
Product types, defining, 51–53
Project charter
defining, 140
team launchers and, 90
Project portfolio, creating an effective
aggregate project plan (APP), role
of, 60–64
development funnel, role of,
65–71
direction setter role and, 48–49
integration of all the parts to
develop, 71–73
portfolio manager role and, 59–65
process creator/owner role and,
65–69
product line architect role and,
50–55, 58–59
Project screens
factors that affect, 67–69
idea generation, 66
idea merging into a single project,
66–67
idea testing and evaluation, 66
resources and commitments
applied, 67
role of, 65–66

Quality through process control,
versus quality inspection, 35
Quantum, 144

Rubbermaid, 1, 2
success and awards given to,
13–14

Screens. *See* Project screens
Second nature (Milestone 4), 156
Senior management
See also Leadership
characteristics of excellent, 28–32
how it can hinder a project, 7–8
implementation and creating the
attitudes and behaviors of,
156–59
role of, in product development,
2–3, 35–36
team building and role of, 79–81,
88, 90–97
timing of management involvment
and influence on product
development, 21–23
views of, when product
development is not considered
critical, 3–5
Senior management, reasons for lack
of involvement by, 34–35
Senior management, reasons for
traditional roles of, 33–35
Silicon Graphics, 72
Soft drink industry, examples of
platform projects, 58
Software develoment, examples of
platform projects, 57–58
Sponsor/coach, teamwork and senior
management's role, 97–98
Sponsor/coach leadership role,
40–41
Support products, 52

Team(s)
activities that ensure that teams
work, 76–77
Chaparral Steel case example,
88–89

Index

Team(s) *(cont.)*
    implementing heavyweight teams
        (Path 1), 139–44
    importance of, 76
    launcher leadership role, 39
    selecting members, 91, 140–41
    support, 141
Team building, stages of
    backing the strategy, 78
    being externally supportive, 79
    "don't rock the boat" stage, 78
    match competitors, 78
    role of senior management, 79–81
Team launcher, tasks of
    creating the contract book, 91–92
    goal establishment, 90
    matching of teams to projects,
        90–91
    selecting team members, 91, 140–41
Teams, role of senior management
        with
    commitment manager, 95–97

    energy source, 92–95
    sponsor/coach, 97–98
    summary of, 99–101
    team launcher, 90–92
Team structures, types of
    advantages and disadvantages of,
        84–86
    autonomous, 84, 85, 86
    functional, 83, 84–85
    heavyweight, 84, 85, 86
    lightweight, 83–84, 85–86
    selecting members for,
        86–87
Timing, product generation map
        and, 55
Toyota, 91

Waffling, 68
Work process, shaping
    in Amalgamated Inc. case example,
        32
    role of, 29

About the Authors

STEVEN C. WHEELWRIGHT is the Class of 1949 Professor of Business Administration at the Harvard Business School. KIM B. CLARK is the first Harry E. Figgie, Jr. Professor of Business Administration at the Harvard Business School. World-renowned experts on technology and product development, they are coauthors of *Revolutionizing Product Development* (Free Press, 1992) and *Dynamic Manufacturing* with Robert H. Hayes (Free Press, 1988).